RIVAL VIEWS
of
MARKET SOCIETY
and Other Recent Essays

Also by Albert O. Hirschman

NATIONAL POWER AND
THE STRUCTURE OF FOREIGN TRADE (1945)

THE STRATEGY OF ECONOMIC DEVELOPMENT (1958)

JOURNEYS TOWARD PROGRESS:
Studies of Economic Policy-Making
in Latin America (1963)

DEVELOPMENT PROJECTS OBSERVED (1967)

EXIT VOICE AND LOYALTY:
Responses to Decline in Firms,
Organizations, and States (1970)

A BIAS FOR HOPE:
Essays on Development and Latin America (1971)

THE PASSIONS AND THE INTERESTS:
Political Arguments for Capitalism
Before Its Triumph (1977)

ESSAYS IN TRESPASSING:
Economics to Politics and Beyond (1981)

SHIFTING INVOLVEMENTS:
Private Interest and Public Action (1982)

GETTING AHEAD COLLECTIVELY:
Grassroots Experiences in Latin America (1984)

RIVAL VIEWS
of
MARKET SOCIETY
and Other Recent Essays

ALBERT O. HIRSCHMAN

ELISABETH SIFTON BOOKS
VIKING

ELISABETH SIFTON BOOKS · VIKING
Viking Penguin Inc., 40 West 23rd Street,
New York, New York 10010, U.S.A.
Penguin Books Ltd, Harmondsworth,
Middlesex, England
Penguin Books Australia Ltd, Ringwood,
Victoria, Australia
Penguin Books Canada Limited, 2801 John Street,
Markham, Ontario, Canada L3R 1B4
Penguin Books (N.Z.) Ltd, 182–190 Wairau Road,
Auckland 10, New Zealand

First published in 1986 by Viking Penguin Inc.
Published simultaneously in Canada

Pages 187–188 constitute an extension of this copyright page.

LIBRARY OF CONGRESS CATALOGING IN PUBLICATION DATA
Hirschman, Albert O.
  Rival views of market society and other recent essays.
  "Elisabeth Sifton books."
  Includes bibliographical references and index.
  1. Economic development. I. Title.
HD75.H57 1986   338.9   85-41076
ISBN 0-670-81319-2

Printed in the United States of America
Set in Primer

Preface

Older folks tend to repeat themselves, but for the aging "academic scribbler" this natural bent is artificially and powerfully reinforced nowadays by insistent demands that he embalm his past thoughts in definitive restatements, that he conveniently sum up, before disappearing, whatever contributions to knowledge he is supposed to have made.

Contemporary pressures of this sort are responsible for the four essays of Part I of the present volume. They originate in requests that I write retrospective or even confessional papers about one or another of the issues with which I once wrestled. Thus the World Bank asked me in 1982 to go over the ideas in economic development I had formulated in the 1950s. Subsequently the enterprising compilers of a new dictionary of economic doctrine and theory invited me to return to concepts I had cultivated at various times, such as interest, linkages in economic development, and exit vs. voice.

In these papers I do summarize my earlier work, but most of the space is devoted to carrying the argument forward and to dealing with a number of new problems that have arisen. The pressures toward self-embalming are, I hope, contained thereby.

The essays in Part II, on rival views of market society and on needed complications in the conceptual structure of economics, could not have been written without my two recent books, *The Passions and the Interests* (1977) and *Shifting Involvements* (1982), respectively. But they are in no way summings-up and, rather, qualify as unexpected and open-ended progeny.

Finally, in Part III, I have gathered some short pieces, most of which are quite speculative and tentative and thus call for elaboration in future years.

All in all, I hope to have vindicated my favorite working title for this collection: "Last Essays, Volume One."

A.O.H.

Princeton, New Jersey
January 1986

Contents

vii

PART I

1. A Dissenter's Confession:

THE STRATEGY OF ECONOMIC DEVELOPMENT REVISITED

Ah, what happened to you, you my written and painted thoughts! Not long ago you were so colorful, young and malicious, so full of thorns and secret spices that you made me sneeze and laugh—and now? Already you have doffed your novelty, and some of you, I fear, are about to become truths: so immortal do they already look, so distressingly honorable, so boring!

—NIETZSCHE

When I received the invitation to participate in this symposium as one of the "pioneers" of development economics alongside Raúl Prebisch, Gunnar Myrdal, Arthur Lewis, and other such luminaries, my first reaction was one of surprise. Not that I doubted my status as a luminary; but, in my own mind, I still saw myself as a rebel against authority, as a second-generation dissenter from the propositions that, while being themselves novel and heterodox, were rapidly shaping up in the 1950s as a new orthodoxy on the problems of development. Had my once daring and insurgent ideas then become classic, respectable, that is, "distressingly honorable" and "boring" in the manner of Nietzsche's plaint? Perhaps. In any event, I must somewhat revise the picture I had

This essay was originally presented at a symposium that brought together retrospective essays by ten economists who, in the judgment of the World Bank, had made "pioneering" contributions to development economics in the 1940s and 1950s. See also Acknowledgments, page 187.

of myself. Viewed in perspective, my dissent, however strong, was in the nature of a demurrer *within* a general movement of ideas attempting to establish development economics as a new field of studies and knowledge.[1] My propositions were at least as distant from the old orthodoxy (later called neoclassical economics) as from the new. In retrospect, therefore, it is only natural that my work should be lumped with the very writings I had chosen as my primary targets.

In an earlier essay,[2] I wrote in the most objective way I could muster about the development of our discipline. To repeat myself as little as possible I shall do the opposite in this paper, which will therefore be totally subjective and self-centered. First, I shall attempt to present the personal backgound and principal motives for the positions I took in *The Strategy of Economic Development.* Next, I shall look at the main propositions I put forward in that book, in the light of subsequent developments and present-day relevance.

DEVELOPING A POINT OF VIEW

There is nothing quite like a good story to lend authority to a half-truth. For a long time, when people asked me how I came to hold the views I proposed in *The Strategy of Economic Development,* my stock answer was: I went to Colombia early in 1952

---

[1]There were other such demurrers. A striking case of convergence with my thinking is Paul Streeten's article "Unbalanced Growth," *Oxford Economic Papers,* n.s., June 1959: 167–90. His article and my book *The Strategy of Economic Development* (whose working title was for a long time "The Economics of Unbalanced Growth") were written quite independently. Paul Streeten tells me that the printing of his article was delayed for several months by a printers' strike, otherwise his defense of unbalanced growth might have come out before mine.

[2]"The Rise and Decline of Development Economics," in *Essays in Trespassing: Economics to Politics and Beyond* (Cambridge University Press, 1981), chap. 1. There will be several references here to this book as well as to *The Strategy of Economic Development* (New Haven, Conn.: Yale University Press, 1958; and New York: Norton, 1978) and to my *A Bias for Hope: Essays on Development and Latin America* (New Haven, Conn.: Yale University Press, 1971). Their titles will here be shortened to, respectively, *Trespassing, Strategy,* and *Bias.*

without any prior knowledge of, or reading about, economic development. This turned out to be a real advantage; I looked at "reality" without theoretical preconceptions of any kind. Then, when I returned to the United States after four and a half years' intensive experience as an official adviser and private consultant, I began to read up on the literature and discovered I had acquired a point of view of my own that was considerably at odds with current doctrines.

It is a nice line, and not *notably* untrue; but now I want to tell a more complex story.

The Marshall Plan Experience and Other Personal Background

I did go to Colombia without being well read in what development literature existed at the time.[3] But I had just been working, with intensity and occasional enthusiasm, on postwar problems of economic reconstruction and cooperation in Western Europe, as an economist with the Federal Reserve Board, from 1946 to 1952. In particular, I had been dealing with economic reconstruction in France and Italy, and with various schemes for European economic integration, such as the European Payments Union, that were central to the Marshall Plan concept.

I came out of this experience with two major impressions or convictions. First, orthodox policy prescriptions for the disrupted postwar economies of Western Europe—stop the inflation and get the exchange rate right—were often politically naive, socially explosive, and economically counterproductive from any long-run point of view. The advocates of orthodoxy seemed to have "forgotten nothing and learned nothing" since the days of the

---

[3] I had participated in one conference on development, held at the University of Chicago in 1951, which was notable primarily for the active participation of some eminent anthropologists and because this was the occasion for Alexander Gerschenkron to unveil his masterpiece, "Economic Backwardness in Historical Perspective." The proceedings of the conference were published as *The Progress of Underdeveloped Areas*, Bert Hoselitz, ed. (University of Chicago Press, 1952), to which I contributed a paper, "Effect of Industrialization on the Markets of Industrial Countries," a topic far removed from development economics as such. The conference stimulated my interest in the problems of development.

Great Depression. And second, the innovators who, to their lasting credit, proposed the creative remedies embodied in the Marshall Plan and, in justification, propounded novel doctrine, such as the "structural dollar shortage," soon became unduly doctrinaire in turn.

These innovators exhibited a perhaps inevitable tendency to take themselves and their ideas too seriously. This was particularly and understandably true for their balance of payments projections, for aid was given in proportion to prospective balance of payments deficits, so that the projections assumed crucial economic and political importance. To be effective advocates within the executive branch and in relations with Congress, we had to exhibit far greater confidence in those statistical estimates than was warranted by the meager extent of our knowledge and foreknowledge, a "dissonant" situation leading to charlatanism in some, and to active dislike of and withdrawal from the whole procedure in others. Moreover, in order to be disavowed as little as possible by emerging reality, Marshall Plan administrators attempted to *make* their estimates come true by taking a considerable interest in the domestic plans and policies that shaped the external accounts of the aid-receiving countries.

During my six years in Washington I sided in general with the innovators, but not without some reservations. From the French and Italian experiences I had lived through in the 1930s, I had come away with a healthy respect (based on watching the misadventures of the French economy) for the efficiency of the price system, particularly with respect to the effect of exchange rate changes on the balance of payments,[4] and with a correlative distrust (based on watching Fascist economic policy in the second half of the 1930s) of peacetime controls, allocations, and grandiloquent plans. Having studied the expansion of Nazi Germany's influence in Eastern and Southeastern Europe, the background to my first book, *National Power and the Structure of Foreign Trade* (1945), I had developed a special sensitivity to the pro-

---

[4]My paper "Devaluation and the Trade Balance: A Note," *Review of Economics and Statistics*, February 1949: 50–53, was a late fruit of that experience.

pensity of large and powerful countries to dominate weaker states through economic transactions. I therefore felt a natural concern and aversion when Marshall Plan administrators were aggressively pressing their views about appropriate domestic programs and policies upon countries such as Italy that were large-scale beneficiaries of aid. They did so for the best of motives—they sincerely sought for Italy not only the "right" balance of payments deficits, but a more prosperous economy and a more equitable society. But it was perhaps because they felt thus unsullied by imperialist concerns that the aid administrators thought they were justified in pursuing their objectives in an imperious manner. Fortunately this phase lasted only a short time, since Marshall Plan aid to Europe was terminated, in surprising accord with the original timetable, after only five years—thereby putting an end also to much of U.S. leverage.

Revolting against a Colombian Assignment

So I went to Colombia with some preconceptions after all. During my first two years there I held the position of economic and financial adviser to the newly established National Planning Council. The World Bank had recommended me for this post, but I worked out a contract directly with the Colombian government. The result was administrative ambiguity that gave me a certain freedom of action. I was in the employ of the Colombian government, but obviously also had some sort of special relationship with the World Bank, which had taken an active part in having the Planning Council set up in the first place and then in recruiting me for it.

My natural inclination, upon taking up my job, was to get myself involved in various concrete problems of economic policy with the intention of learning as much as possible about the Colombian economy and in the hope of contributing marginally to the improvement of policy-making. But word soon came from World Bank headquarters that I was principally expected to take the initiative, as soon as possible, in formulating some ambitious economic development plan that would spell out investment, domestic savings, growth, and foreign aid targets for the Colombian economy over the next few years. All of this was alleged to be quite simple for experts mastering the new programming technique: apparently there now existed adequate knowledge, even without close study of local surroundings, of the likely ranges of savings and capital-output ratios, and those estimates, joined to the country's latest national income and balance of payments accounts, would yield all the key figures needed. I resisted being relegated to this sort of programming activity. Having already plunged into some of the country's real problems, I felt that one of the things Colombia needed least was a synthetic development plan compiled on the basis of "heroic" estimates. This was a repetition, under much less favorable circumstances (the quality of the numbers was much poorer), of what I had most disliked about work on the Marshall Plan.

One aspect of this affair made me particularly uneasy. The task was supposedly crucial for Colombia's development, yet no Colombian was to be found who had any inkling of how to go about it. That knowledge was held only by a few foreign experts who had had the new growth economics revealed to them. It all seemed to be an affront to the Colombians who were, after all, struggling or tinkering with their problems in many fields through a great variety of private decisions and public policies. My instinct was to try to understand better *their* patterns of action, rather than assume from the outset that they could be "developed" only by importing a set of techniques they knew nothing about. True, this paternalistic mode of operation was given much encouragement by the Colombians themselves, who were, initially at least, treating the foreign advisers as a new brand of magicians, and who loved to pour scorn on themselves by exclaiming at every opportunity, *"Aquí en el trópico hacemos todo al revés"* (Here in the tropics we do everything the wrong way around). But the foreign advisers and experts took such statements far too literally. Many Colombians did not really feel all that inept. For at least some of them the phrase implied that, in the particular environment in which they operated, they might well have worked out by trial and error some cunning principles of action, of which they were themselves hardly conscious, that might seem perverse to outsiders, but have actually proven quite effective.

SEARCHING FOR HIDDEN RATIONALITIES

This was exactly what I thought worth exploring. I began to look for elements and processes of the Colombian reality that *did* work, perhaps in roundabout and unappreciated fashion. Far more fundamentally than the idea of unbalanced growth, this search for possible *hidden rationalities* was to give an underlying unity to my work. It also gave it vulnerability.

To uncover the hidden rationality of seemingly odd, irrational, or reprehensible social behavior has been an important and quite respectable pastime of social scientists ever since Mandeville and Adam Smith. (In the humanities, the tradition goes much further back, at least to Erasmus's *Praise of Folly*.) If successful, the search results in those "typically counterintuitive, shocking" discoveries on which social science thrives.[5]

My principal findings of this kind were the possible rationality ("uses") of (1) shortages, bottlenecks, and other unbalanced growth sequences in the course of development; (2) capital-intensive industrial processes; and (3) the pressures on decision makers caused by inflation and balance of payments deficits. These were the key themes of *The Strategy of Economic Development* and I shall discuss them later. But I must say something right away about the vulnerability that comes with such discoveries.

Once the discoveries were made and proudly exhibited, there arose, inevitably and embarrassingly, the question: Would you actually *advocate* unbalanced growth, capital-intensive investment, inflation, and so on? The honest, if a bit unsatisfactory,

---

[5]See "Morality and the Social Sciences: A Durable Tension," in *Trespassing*, chapter 14, p. 298.

answer must be: yes, but of course within some fairly strict limits. There is no doubt that the unbalanced growth strategy can be overdone, with dire consequences. But I stand by the concluding paragraph of an article I wrote jointly with C. E. Lindblom to bring out the similarity of our approaches in different fields:

> There are limits to "imbalance" in economic development, to "lack of integration" in research and development, to "fragmentation" in policy making which would be dangerous to pass. And it is clearly impossible to specify in advance the optimal doses of these various policies under different circumstances. The art of promoting economic development, research and development, and constructive policy making in general consists, then, in acquiring a feeling for those doses. This art . . . will be mastered far better once the false ideals of "balance," "coordination," and "comprehensive overview" have lost our total and unquestioning intellectual allegiance.[6]

Another problem arises in connection with that embarrassing question about advocacy. Social scientists who discover the hidden rationality of a social practice should be aware that they frequently act as something of a spoilsport: once the uses of unbalanced growth or of inflation are discovered and explained, the attempt consciously to apply these notions and to replicate the earlier successes is likely to stumble for various reasons. For one, policymakers who up to then had merely backed into such devices will now tend to overdo and otherwise abuse the newly discovered knowledge.[7] Moreover, various affected parties will neutralize much of the policy by acting in anticipation of it once it is expected, in line with reasoning made familiar by the rational-expectations argument.

Thus the discovery of hidden rationalities clearly yields "dangerous knowledge." But, as is well known, knowledge is intrinsically dangerous. And this simple observation gives me a chance to turn the tables on my critics. As long as the findings I had

---

[6]From "Economic Development, Research and Development, Policy Making: Some Converging Views" (1962), reprinted in *Bias*, pp. 83–84.

[7]I noted this previously for the combination of inflation and overvaluation which permitted the financing of import-substituting industrialization in many countries in the 1950s. See *Trespassing*, p. 110.

come up with were dangerous, there was at least some chance that they truly constituted new knowledge. This is more than can be said for quite a few of the bland and banal pieties that have been paraded under the banner of either "principles of development planning" or "efficient allocation of resources"!

Uncovering hidden rationalities permitted me to fight against what I perceived as two very different yet interrelated evils. On the one hand, I reacted against the visiting-economist syndrome; that is, against the habit of issuing peremptory advice and prescription by calling on universally valid economic principles and remedies—be they old or brand new—after a strictly minimal acquaintance with the "patient." But, with time, another objective was assuming even more importance in my mind: it was to counter the tendency of many Colombians and Latin Americans to work hand in glove with the visiting economist by their own self-deprecatory attitudes. As I put it in a subsequent article, "Some of my main contentions could serve to reconcile the Latin Americans with their reality, to assure them that certain ubiquitous phenomena such as bottlenecks and imbalances in which they see the constantly renewed proof of their ineptness and inferiority are on the contrary inevitable concomitants and sometimes even useful stimulants of development."[8]

Because Latin Americans were wont to issue blanket condemnations of their reality, they became incapable of learning from their own experiences, so it seemed to me. Later, in detailed studies of economic policy-making, I even coined a term for this trait: the "failure complex," or *fracasomania* in Spanish and Portuguese.[9]

At this point, however, my bias for hidden rationalities might seem to harbor yet another danger. Was it not going to make me

---

[8]"Ideologies of Economic Development in Latin America," first published in 1961 and reprinted in *Bias,* pp. 310–11.

[9]See my *Journeys toward Progress: Studies of Economic Policy Making in Latin America* (New York: Twentieth Century Fund, 1963; Norton, 1973); and "Policymaking and Policy Analysis in Latin America—A Return Journey" (1974), reprinted in *Trespassing.* In both works, but particularly in the latter, I pointed out that *fracasomania* (the failure complex) could lead to real *fracasos* (failures).

blind to the imperative need for change in societies where economic growth was frustrated at every turn by antiquated institutions and attitudes as well as by exorbitant privilege? Was my
enterprise then going to end up as a giant exercise in apology
for the existing order (or disorder)? This danger actually never
bothered me much, for the simple reason that the hidden rationalities I was after were precisely and principally *processes of growth
and change already under way* in the societies I studied, processes that were often unnoticed by the actors immediately involved, as well as by foreign experts and advisers. I was not
looking for reasons to justify what was, but for reasons to think
that the old order was always changing. In this way I tried to
identify progressive economic and political forces that deserved
recognition and help. This position did put me at odds with those
who judged that the present society was "rotten through and
through" and that nothing would ever change unless everything
was changed at once. But this utopian dream of the "visiting
revolutionary" seemed to me of a piece with the balanced growth
and integrated development schemes of the visiting economist.[10]

A Paradigm of My Own?

My basic concern with the discovery of hidden rationality
shows up in my first general paper on development, written in
1954 after two years in Colombia, for a conference on Investment
Criteria and Economic Growth at the Massachusetts Institute of
Technology.[11] Here I presented, besides a critique of what I called
"The Myth of Integrated Investment Planning," two empirical
observations which could qualify as investment criteria. One was
about the superior performance of airplanes in comparison with
highways in Colombia (the need for adequate maintenance and
efficient performance in general being far more compelling in
the case of airplanes), a point which later led me to a general
hypothesis about the comparative advantage less developed coun-

---

[10]For some elaboration, see *Journeys*, pp. 251–56.
[11]Reprinted in *Bias*.

tries have in certain types of activities. The other observation dealt with what I then described as "the impact of secondary on primary production" and later named "backward linkage." Both observations served to justify investments (in the case of airlines) or investment sequences (in the case of backward linkage) that seemed questionable or *al revés* (the wrong way around) from the commonsense point of view.

In 1954 these were isolated observations. But they remained key elements of the conceptual structure that I erected three years or so later in *The Strategy of Economic Development*. I now searched for a general economic principle that would tie them (and several related propositions) together. To this end, I suggested that underdeveloped countries need special "pressure mechanisms" or "pacing devices" to bring forth their potential. In my most general formulation I wrote: "development depends not so much on finding optimal combinations for given resources and factors of production as on calling forth and enlisting for development purposes resources and abilities that are hidden, scattered, or badly utilized."

I presented this point as a special characteristic of the underdeveloped countries and implicitly granted that the advanced countries continued to be ruled by the traditional principles of maximization and optimization, on the basis of given and known resources and factors of production. Actually, these principles were to be impugned in short order, or were already being impugned, precisely for the advanced countries, by various important contributions of other economists. For the business firm, Richard Cyert and James March documented the importance of what they called "organizational slack," on the basis of Herbert Simon's pioneering work on "satisficing" as opposed to "maximizing." Adopting the concept of "inducement mechanism," Nathan Rosenberg showed how the pattern of inventions and innovations in the advanced countries simply does not follow the gradual expansion of opportunities as markets and knowledge grow, but has been strongly influenced by special "inducing" or "focusing" events such as strikes and wars. Finally, Harvey Leibenstein built his X-efficiency theory on the notion that slack is ubiquitous and effort sporadic and unreliable, again in the absence of special pressure situations.[12]

It appears, therefore, that the very characteristics on which I had sought to build an economics specially attuned to the underdeveloped countries have a far wider, perhaps even a universal, range and that they define, not a special strategy of development for a well-defined group of countries, but a much more generally valid approach to the understanding of change and growth. In other words, I set out to learn about others, and in the end learned about ourselves.

As many anthropologists have discovered and taught us, this is by no means an unusual meandering of social thought and knowledge. Nor does it come to me as a disappointment that I must give up the pretense of having discovered *the* distinguishing characteristic of underdeveloped societies. There always was some irony, not to say inconsistency, in the intellectual path I followed. First I rejected the old and new paradigms of others and stressed the importance of steeping oneself in the Colombian reality— from which I eventually emerged with a triumphant paradigm of my own! So I am quite happy at this point to renounce that claim, especially as long as some of my more specific findings and suggestions (frequently generated only by means of my overall conceptual scheme) continue to lead an active life of their own. I shall now show that this is indeed the case.

(In order not to be misunderstood I must emphasize that I do not renounce my basic idea—about the need for pacing devices and so on—but only the claim that with it I had hit upon the *distinguishing* characteristic of a certain group of economically less developed countries.)

---

[12]H. A. Simon, "A Behavioral Model of Rational Choice," *Quarterly Journal of Economics,* February 1955: 99–118; Richard M. Cyert and James G. March, *Behavioral Theory of the Firm* (Englewood Cliffs, N.J.: Prentice-Hall, 1963); Nathan Rosenberg, "The Direction of Technological Change: Inducement Mechanisms and Focusing Devices," *Economic Development and Cultural Change,* October 1969: 18; and Harvey Leibenstein, "Allocative Efficiency versus X-Efficiency," *American Economic Review,* June 1966: 392–415, and *Beyond Economic Man* (Cambridge, Mass.: Harvard University Press, 1976).

THE LIFE OF
SOME SPECIFIC PROPOSITIONS

Linkages

If a popularity contest were held for the various propositions I advanced in *Strategy*, the idea of favoring industries with strong backward and forward linkages would surely receive first prize. The linkage concept has achieved the ultimate success: it is by now so much part of the language of development economics that its procreator is most commonly no longer mentioned when it is being invoked.

I fought a major battle against the then widely alleged need for a "balanced" or "big push" industrialization effort; that is, against the idea that industrialization could be successful only if it were undertaken as a large-scale effort, carefully planned on many fronts simultaneously. To contradict this idea I pointed to the processes of industrialization that could in fact be observed in Colombia and other developing countries. Their entrepreneurs, domestic and foreign, had apparently hit upon a good number of *sequential* rather than *simultaneous* solutions to the problem of industrialization, but the more typical sequences were often unusual by the standards of experience in the more advanced countries. Precisely for this reason, these sequences either were not easily perceived or, once noted, were judged to be characteristic of an inferior, ineffficient, or (according to a term that became fashionable in the 1960s) "dependent" industrialization.

My approach was exactly the opposite. Following Gerschenkron, I saw originality and creativity in deviating from the path followed by the older industrial countries, in skipping stages, and in inventing sequences that had a "wrong way around" look. It was surely this attitude that permitted me to ferret out the backward and forward linkage dynamic and to acclaim as a dialectical-paradoxical feat what was later called, with disparaging intent,[13] import-substituting industrialization: in its course, a country would

---

[13]*Trespassing*, p. 127, n. 39.

acquire a comparative advantage in the goods it imports; for the "fatter" the imports of a given consumer good grew, the greater was the likelihood that, in Hansel and Gretel fashion, they would be "devoured" or "swallowed" by a newly established domestic industry. My intent throughout was to underline the originality of these various dynamics, as well as the feasibility, then in doubt, of a sequential approach. As with unbalanced growth, there was of course danger that the dynamics I celebrated could be overdone, to the point of setting up a highly inefficient industrial structure. But is it not unreasonable to ask the inventor of the internal combustion engine to come up immediately with a design for pollution control and air bags?

Be that as it may, as an analytic tool the linkages have led an active life over the past twenty-five years. They have been particularly useful in orienting various historical studies of developing economies.[14] It has been much more difficult to turn the linkage criterion (priority to investment in industries with strong linkage effects) into an operational device for industrial planning, with the help of input-output statistics. A great deal of discussion about appropriate measurement has taken place.[15] The most extensive and successful study of this sort to date has been undertaken by the Regional Employment Program for Latin America and the Caribbean (PREALC) of the International Labor Office.[16] It uses the linkage concept for the purpose of meas-

---

[14]Albert Fishlow, *American Railroads and the Transformation of the Ante-Bellum Economy* (Cambridge, Mass.: Harvard University Press, 1965); Judith Tendler, *Electric Power in Brazil: Entrepreneurship in the Public Sector* (Cambridge, Mass.: Harvard University Press, 1968); Michael Roemer, *Fishing for Growth: Export-led Development in Peru, 1959–1967* (Cambridge, Mass.: Harvard University Press, 1970); Scott R. Pearson, *Petroleum and the Nigerian Economy* (Stanford University Press, 1970); and Richard Weisskoff and Edward Wolff, "Linkages and Leakages: Industrial Tracking in an Enclave Economy," *Economic Development and Cultural Change,* July 1977: 607–28.

[15]See the symposium on linkage effect measurement in *Quarterly Journal of Economics,* May 1976: 308–43.

[16]Norberto E. García and Manuel Marfán, "Estructuras industriales y eslabonamientos de empleo" [Industrial structures and employment linkages], Monografía sobre empleo 126 (Santiago: PREALC, December 1982).

uring employment creation, rather than industrial expansion in terms of value added. The idea is of course to help in devising an industrialization strategy that would maximize employment. One empirical finding of the study deserves special notice: once the indirect employment effects (via backward and forward linkages) are taken into account, investment in large-scale (capital-intensive) industry turns out to be just as employment-creating as investment in small-scale (labor-intensive) industry for the industrially advanced countries of Latin America.

The linkage concept was devised for a better understanding of the industrialization process, and initially most applications were in this area. Fairly soon, however, the concept caught on even more in the analysis of the growth patterns of developing countries during the phase when their principal engine of growth was (or is) the export of primary products.[17] Very different growth paths were traced out by countries exporting copper rather than coffee, and these differences were difficult to explain by the traditional macroeconomic variables. The linkages permitted a more detailed look, yet stopped short of the wholly descriptive account that had been practiced by Harold Innis and other practitioners of the so-called staple thesis.

At this point the linkage concept proliferated. In analogy to backward and forward linkage, consumption linkage was defined as the process by which the new incomes of the primary producers lead first to imports of consumer goods and then—in line with the "swallowing" dynamic—to their replacement by domestic (industrial or agricultural) production. Similarly, fiscal linkage is said to occur when the state taxes the newly accruing incomes for the purpose of financing investments elsewhere in the economy. Such fiscal linkages are either direct, as when the state is able to siphon off a portion of exporters' profits through export duties or royalties, or indirect—in this case the various incomes earned through exports are not tapped directly, but are

---

[17]For a more extensive treatment of this topic, see "A Generalized Linkage Approach to Development, with Special Reference to Staples," in *Trespassing.*

allowed to generate a flow of imports which are then made to yield fiscal revenue through tariffs.

Once the various ways through which exports of primary products can give rise to further economic activities had come into view, it became clear that some of the linkages are usually to be had only at the cost of doing without some of the others. In this manner, typical *constellations* of linkages could be identified for different kinds of primary commodities; as a result, it became possible to differentiate what had long been designated "export-led growth" and treated as a unified and transparent process. More important still, this approach almost compels one to consider the interaction between the social structure and the state, on the one hand, and the more narrowly economic factors, on the other.

Latitude in Performance Standards

While the linkages, in their increasingly numerous varieties, help us understand how one thing leads to another in economic development, an even more basic inquiry is how one firm or productive operation can be made to *endure* as an efficiently performing unit of the economic system. The answer to this question yielded what was, in my opinion—and, once again, in that of any market test—the other major find I made in Colombia. It had its origin in the already noted observation about the comparative efficiency (and maintenance) of airplanes and highways and developed into the much more general point—sometimes called the Hirschman hypothesis—contrasting machine-paced with operator-paced machinery, and process-centered with product-centered industrial activities.[18] An implication was that a cer-

---

[18]The hypothesis lent itself to testing by empirical data; if it were true, the productivity differentials between advanced and less developed countries would be larger in certain types of industries than in others. A large number of attempts at testing have been made and are reviewed in Simon Teitel, "Productivity, Mechanization, and Skills: A Test of the Hirschman Hypothesis for Latin American Industry," *World Development,* 1981: 355–71. See also M. Shahid Alam, "Hirschman's Taxonomy of Industries: Some Hypotheses and Evidence," *Economic Development and Cultural Change,* January 1984: 367–72.

tain type of capital-intensive, advanced technology could be more appropriate, in a country with little industrial tradition, than the labor-intensive technology and "idiot-proof" machinery—contrary to some of the most frequent, automatic, and insistent advice proffered by visiting experts.

I became fascinated with this point for several reasons. First, it permitted me to indicate another hidden rationality: the widely noted preference of developing countries for advanced technology and capital-intensive industry with a flow process was perhaps not in all cases a damaging bias, based exclusively on misguided prestige-seeking.

Second, I had come upon a concept or criterion that was helpful in understanding a number of social and economic processes: the greater or smaller extent of latitude in standards of performance (or tolerance for poor performance) as a characteristic inherent in all production tasks. When this latitude is narrow the corresponding task has to be performed *just right;* otherwise, it cannot be performed at all or is exposed to an unacceptable level of risk (for example, high probability of crash in the case of poorly maintained or poorly operated airplanes). Lack of latitude therefore brings powerful pressures for efficiency, quality performance, good maintenance habits, and so on. It thus substitutes for inadequately formed motivations and attitudes, which will be *induced* and generated by the narrow-latitude task instead of presiding over it.

Here, then, was another promising "wrong way around" sequence. Ever since Max Weber, many social scientists looked at the "right" cultural attitudes and beliefs as necessary conditions ("prerequisites") for economic progress, just as earlier theories had emphasized race, climate, or the presence of natural resources. In the 1950s, newly fashioned cultural theories of development competed strongly with the economic ones (which stressed capital formation), with Weber's Protestant Ethic being modernized into David McClelland's "achievement motivation" as a preconditon of progress and into Edward C. Banfield's "amoral familism" as an obstacle. According to my way of thinking, the very attitudes alleged to be preconditions of industrialization could

be generated on the job and "on the way," by certain characteristics of the industrialization process.[19]

The emphasis on latitude in performance standards as a variable influencing efficiency also had a bearing on approaches that
regard certain economic institutions as necessary conditions for
development. For many economists, competition is the all-powerful social institution bringing pressures for efficiency. Strangely
and somewhat inconsistently, some of these economists seem
intent on granting competition a monopoly in this endeavor. But
with competition being so often quite feeble and with the battle
against inefficiency and decay being so generally uphill, why not
search and be grateful for additional mechanisms that, to para-
phrase Rousseau, force man to be efficient? Lack of latitude
seemed to me to hold considerable promise in this regard. Twelve
years later I stressed another such mechanism: protests, complaints, and criticism by consumers and, more generally, by members of organizations when the quality of the organization's output
deteriorates. This I called "voice," and the interaction of voice
with competition, called "exit" for greater generality, involved me
in the writing of another book, *Exit, Voice, and Loyalty* (1970).

One matter I notice only now, with much surprise over the
underlying unity of my thought: there appears to be a real affinity
between these two mechanisms, which I developed quite independently one from the other. Narrow-latitude tasks will, if performed poorly and (ex hypothesi) disastrously, give rise to strong
public concern and outcry—to voice. This is obvious in the case
of airplane crashes, and I specifically noted it in *Strategy* for
another concrete example of a narrow-latitude task, road construction using a certain technology. I cited the opinion of a
highway engineer who favored cheap bituminous surfaces on
little traveled routes, rather than gravel and stone surfaces, for
the reason that, as he wrote to me, "local pressure would be
applied to the Ministry of Public Works to repair the deep holes

---

[19]See also Alex Inkeles and David H. Smith, *Becoming Modern* (Cambridge,
Mass.: Harvard University Press, 1974).

which will develop in cheap bituminous surfaces if maintenance and retreatment are delayed, and that such pressure would be greater than if a gravel and stone road is allowed to deteriorate." Maintenance of cheap bituminous surfaces is therefore a narrow-latitude task that, if neglected, is likely to give rapid rise to strong voice (the results of poor performance being intolerable).

It could be argued that, in this case and in that of airplanes, voice is the only available mechanism, since these are instances of natural or institutional monopoly (in the case of air transportation being reserved to one national airline). This is not so, however; even when competition is lively for narrow-latitude products or services—for example, pharmaceuticals—public regulation is generally present, testifying to the presence of public concern and to the feeling that, because of the possibly disastrous consequences, the assurance of the "right" level of quality cannot be left to market forces. I had earlier pointed out that voice is likely to come to the fore when there is a strong public interest— for example, because of concerns for health and safety.[20] The narrow-latitude criterion leads to the same conclusion.

If there is a strong affinity between narrow-latitude and voice, one would expect a corresponding association between exit (that is, competition) and wide-latitude goods and services. These are items that can be and are produced and marketed to very different quality standards, without lower quality having disastrous effects. It is indeed correct that, with regard to such goods and services, comparison shopping and competition in general come peculiarly into their own. The attractiveness of Milton Friedman's proposal for introducing competition into primary and secondary education may precisely derive from the wide-latitude characteristic of education. It is a fact that the quality of education varies widely and that this variability is both inevitable (because of varying teacher quality, for one) and tolerated by the public, however disastrous the individual and social effects of poor education may in fact be. On this score, then, I must grant that education seems

---

[20]See *Trespassing*, p. 217.

to be a task whose performance might be improved by compe-tition. For reasons I have discussed elsewhere,[21] however, the maintenance and improvement of quality in education still seem to me to require, on balance, a strong admixture of voice.

Even before I came to write on exit and voice, the concept of lack of tolerance for poor performance continued to yield div-idends. In my *Development Projects Observed* (1967), a chapter entitled "Latitudes and Disciplines" deals with the many pres-sures for performance stemming from various characteristics of a specific project: spatial or locational latitude, temporal discipline in construction, tolerance for corruption, latitude in substituting quantity for quality, and so on. These categories proved quite useful in understanding the specific difficulties and accomplish-ments of different projects.

Later I found that I was by no means the inventor of these concepts of latitude or discipline and of their uses, but that I had some illustrious predecessors, such as Montesquieu and Sir James Steuart! These thinkers were evidently not concerned with the functioning of development projects or the efficiency of industry; they had more portentous matters on their mind—their overrid-ing concern was the more or less tolerable performance of the state. But here their reasoning was very close to mine; they were looking for ways of constraining the latitude of the state, of re-pressing the "passions" of the sovereign, and they thought they found a solution in the expansion of the "interests" and the mar-ket. I shall not retell this tale here, but merely mean to indicate the straightforward connection between my interest in the com-parative performance of airlines and highways in Colombia and the principal theme of my book *The Passions and the Interests* (1977). Here, also, I came up against the limits of latitude con-cept, but that is another story.

Inflation and Balance of Payments Problems
One of the pleasant experiences in writing a book rather than an article is that the ideas one starts out with are given enough

---

[21]See *Trespassing*, pp. 219–22.

breathing space so they can fully unfold and expand in all kinds of originally unanticipated directions. This is what happened with *Strategy*. The book's basic theses on unbalanced growth and sequential problem-solving eventually yielded positions of my own on the problems of inflation, balance of payments disequilibrium, and population pressures, as well as on regional development. In the following I shall limit myself to just two of these topics.[22]

With its shortages and bottlenecks, the unbalanced development path I had described as most typical "conveys an almost physical sensation of inflationary shocks being administered to an economy." Relative price rises, so I argued, play an important role, via more or less elastic supply responses, in overcoming the imbalances. In the process, however, "with any given level of skill and determination of [the] monetary and fiscal managers" the general price level will be subject to upward pressure, especially if supply responses are weak or slow in some key sectors such as food and foreign exchange. In this manner, I put forward a view on inflation that was just then being elaborated within the UN Economic Commission for Latin America as the "structuralist," as opposed to the "monetarist," approach. That very view came to the fore in the North, without any reference to its Southern antecedents, of course, under the name of "supply-shock inflation" during the oil crises of the 1970s and their monetary repercussions.[23]

In presenting inflation as the unfortunate but to-be-expected side effect of a certain type of growth process, I had in mind the

---

[22]At the time my book appeared, my most "scandalous" position was the one I expressed on population pressures. I maintained that, in certain circumstances, such pressures could be considered as stimulants rather than as depressants of development. I do not wish to return to the argument here, except to point out that my position was later given considerable support through the influential writings of Ester Boserup, who stressed the effects of population growth on the introduction of new agricultural techniques. See her books *The Conditions of Agricultural Growth* (New York: Aldine, 1965), and, more recently, *Population and Technological Change* (University of Chicago Press, 1981).

[23]An extended retrospective treatment of these matters is in my survey article, "The Social and Political Matrix of Inflation: Elaborations on the Latin American Experience," in *Trespassing,* chapter 8.

comparatively moderate inflations—in the 20 to 30 percent range—
that Colombia and Brazil were experiencing in the 1950s. I advocated implicitly a greater comprehension on the part of the
advanced countries and the international financial institutions
(the International Monetary Fund and the World Bank), which
at that time considered any two-digit inflation as evidence of
profligate fiscal and monetary policies that had to be corrected
before further development finance was made available. Particularly in the Brazil of the Kubitschek years this policy seemed to
me highly ill-advised, and I still believe that it bears some responsibility for the tragic "derailment" of Brazilian politics from
1958 to the military takeover in 1964.[24] This brings me to the
balance of payments problems of developing countries. Once again
I analyzed pressures on a country's international accounts as
"part and parcel of the process of unbalanced growth" rather
than as primarily the reflection of macroeconomic disequilibrium
between domestic savings and investments. In this perspective,
the needs of developing countries for international financial assistance arise not so much from the fact that they are too poor
to save the amounts needed to achieve some growth target—this
was the then current rationale for foreign aid—as from some
disproportionalities that arise in the growth process. At some
stage the need of the expanding economy for imported inputs
outpaces its ability to increase exports, unless the country is lucky
enough to produce some items that are in rapidly expanding
demand on the world market. In other words, the need for financial assistance from abroad would by no means be greatest
when the country is poorest, but would be likely to bulge—perhaps several times—in the course of development as certain initially import-intensive economic activities are being put into place.
The point was once again to get away from the excessive sim-
plicities of certain growth models and to argue that balance of

---

[24]For a critical evaluation of World Bank policy in Brazil during the 1950s,
see Edward S. Mason and Robert E. Asher, *The World Bank since Bretton Woods*
(Washington, D.C.: Brookings Institution, 1973), pp. 660–62.

payments pressures, like inflation, are not necessarily reflections of profligate fiscal and monetary policies.

So much for the effect of growth on the balance of payments. How about the equally important inverse relation—the effect of foreign-exchange abundance or stringency on growth? Here I put forward an idea,[25] which I have since used in a number of increasingly broad contexts, based on a simple observation: after a period of comparative foreign-exchange *affluence* that causes certain consumption habits, based on imports, to take root, the experience of foreign-exchange *shortage* has often set in motion industrial investments designed to produce the previously imported goods that are now sorely missed; it therefore looked as though some alternation of good and hard times (with regard to foreign exchange availability) could be particularly effective in fostering industrial development. I made a similar point with regard to regional development: I saw certan advantages in an underdeveloped region (such as northeastern Brazil) being closely integrated with the country's more advanced provinces, whereas other kinds of development stimuli would arise from withdrawal and insulation. Later on, I wrote about the virtues of *some* oscillation between contact and insulation in connection with both foreign trade and investment.[26]

This thesis was not going to make me popular with either the advocates of delinking or their neoclassical opponents.[27] Once again, moreover, it was sure to disappoint those looking for operational policy advice: first, the optimal width of the oscillation between foreign-exchange affluence and penury is impossible to define; second, such ups and downs are generally not subject to

---

[25]I originally expressed the idea in a discussion paper written for a conference of the International Economic Association held at Rio in 1957. See Howard S. Ellis, ed., *Economic Development for Latin America* (New York: St. Martin's Press, 1961), p. 460; and *Strategy*, pp. 173–76.

[26]See *Bias*, pp. 25 and 229–30.

[27]An excellent survey of the pros and cons of delinking is in Carlos F. Diaz Alejandro, "Delinking North and South: Unshackled or Unhinged?" in Albert Fishlow et al., *Rich and Poor Nations in the World Economy* (New York: McGraw-Hill, 1978), pp. 87–162.

a single country's control. If it is correct, my point nevertheless has important implications: it makes policymakers aware that each situation brings with it its own set of opportunities (and of possible calamities).

The principle of oscillation is obviously a close relative of the strategy of unbalanced growth—a topic on which I have some new thoughts.

The Politics of Unbalanced Growth

To write in praise of lack of balance is evidently a provocation for which a price must be paid. The worst penalty is inflicted not by the critics, but by those who proclaim themselves devoted disciples and commit all kinds of horrors in one's name.

Here is a striking example of this sort of occurrence. On a visit to Argentina around 1968, shortly after the military coup that toppled the civilian regime of Illia and brought to power General Onganía, I was told by a high-ranking official, "All we are doing is applying your ideas of unbalanced growth. In Argentina we cannot achieve all our political, social, and economic objectives at once; therefore we have decided to proceed by stages, as though in an unbalanced growth sequence. First we must straighten out the economic problems, that is, restore economic stability and stimulate growth; thereafter, we will look out for greater social equity; and only then will the country be ready for a restoration of civil liberties and for other political advances." I was of course appalled by this "application" of my ideas. It seemed quite preposterous to me on various counts. After all, the imbalances I had written about were far less grand than those referred to by my Argentine interlocutor. They had been confined to the economic sphere and were concerned with disproportionalities between sectors, such as industry and agriculture, and even more with interactions between much more finely subdivided subsectors. Because of the interdependence of the economy in the input-output sense, the expansion of one sector or subsector ahead of the other could be relied on to set forces in motion (relative price changes and public policies in response to complaints about shortages) that would tend to eliminate the initial imbalance. As

I put it in a letter written in 1959 to André Gunder Frank, who wrote one of the more perceptive reviews of my book[28] (this was before his "development-of-underdevelopment" phase):

> If one wants to move [straight] from one equilibrium position to the next, then, because of the discontinuities and invisibilities *that I take for granted,* the "big push" or "minimum critical effort" is indispensable. But if we assume that intermediate positions of development-stimulating disequilibrium are sustainable at least for limited time periods, then we can manage to break down the big push into a series of smaller steps. In other words, I am in favor of utilizing the energy which holds together economic nuclei of given minimum size in the *building up* of these nuclei.

In addition to making clear my position as dissent from a dissent without a return to the original orthodoxy, this passage well expresses my conception of the unbalanced growth process as something fueled and justified by the "energy which holds together" the various sectors and branches of the economy and which would ensure that the various imbalances would be approximately self-correcting.

Even for intersectoral imbalances, my principal concern was not so much to praise imbalance in general as to draw a distinction between "compulsive" and merely "permissive" sequences. On the basis of this distinction, I was critical of the then prevailing emphasis on investments in infrastructure. Further, I noted that in regional development the process of unbalanced growth is fundamentally different from unbalanced growth in the sectoral sense because of the weakness of the forces making for restoration of interregional balance. Hence, it is illegitimate to invoke the unbalanced-growth idea when there are no compelling reasons why an advance in one direction and the ensuing imbalance should set countervailing forces in motion. In the Argentine case I have cited, it was impossible to detect any such forces unless one trusted the self-proclaimed intentions of the new regime (that came duly to naught) or the dubious correlations between eco-

---

[28]"Built-in Destabilization: A. O. Hirschman's Strategy of Economic Development," *Economic Development and Cultural Change,* July 1960: 433–40.

nomic growth and the growth of democracy adduced by the more sanguine political-development theorists of the time.

But there is another, perhaps more interesting, way in which the Argentine sequence differed from the one I had talked about. My Argentine interlocutor conveniently failed to menton that the military had just ordered severe curtailments of political freedoms. Whatever economic advance the new regime would bring was being achieved at the cost of previously political and civil rights of the citizens. Later on these rights were to be restored— perhaps, in turn, at the cost of some of the previous economic advances? This sort of (implicit) sequence is again very different from the one I had had in mind: in my scheme one sector, say, manufacturing industry, was to move ahead without any simultaneous expansion in power or transportation or agriculture, but certainly not at the expense of these sectors. Nevertheless, there is here some scope for reflection and, at long last, for self-criticism. Is it really true that the process of unbalanced growth never implies actual retrogression for any economic agents? Probably not. When industry advances and uses the *existing* power and transportation facilities, then, in the absence of excess capacity, there are fewer such facilities available for the traditional users, who will therefore be worse off. The same is likely to hold, with rather more serious consequences, for an isolated advance of industry while agricultural output remains stationary.[29]

It appears therefore that, for some of these purposes, I have to redraw the diagram by which I attempted to portray the unbalanced-growth process.[30] The comparatively innocuous pattern of figure 1 is transformed by the preceding considerations into

---

[29]This matter could obviously be elaborated at considerable length. The effect of unbalanced growth on sectoral incomes in a two- or three-sector economy depends on the intersectoral terms of trade, and it is conceivable that the incomes generated in the expanding sector would decline rather than expand. Harry G. Johnson's classic article, "Economic Expansion and International Trade," is still a good starting point for the analysis of the various possibilities. See *Manchester School of Economic and Social Studies,* May 1955: 96–101.

[30]The most straightforward such presentation is in "Economic Development, Research and Development, and Policy Making: Some Converging Views," p. 65; in *Strategy* a similar, but more complex, diagram is on p. 87.

Figure 1. *Balanced and Unbalanced Growth*

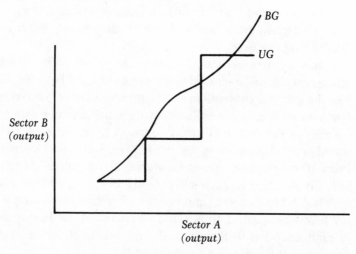

Figure 2. *Antagonistic Growth*

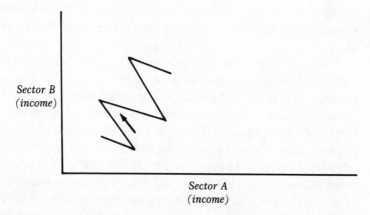

the more problematic pattern of figure 2, where at each stage in the sequential growth process the income receivers of one of the two sectors are gaining at the expense of those of the other sector. As drawn, to reflect the eventual all-around increases in output, the incomes received in both sectors are growing in the course of the process as a whole, but at any one point Sector A is gaining at the expense of Sector B or vice versa, making for what might be called an *antagonistic* growth process. Note that antagonistic is very different from zero-sum, since all-around growth is in effect being achieved.

I had not noticed that my unbalanced growth path had these antagonistic implications. Had I done so I might have inquired into the political consequences and prerequisites of the process. For it to unfold, a certain level of tolerance for increasing inequality in the course of growth appears to be required. I later investigated this matter in my article "The Tolerance for Income Inequality in the Course of Economic Development" (1973),[31] but only after the antagonistic potential of the development process had led to civil wars and various other disasters. Along with my fellow pioneers, I thus stand convicted of not having paid enough attention to the political implications of the economic development theories we propounded.[32]

But perhaps it was not altogether unfortunate that we were myopic and parochial. Had we been more farsighted and interdisciplinary, we might have recoiled from advocating any action whatever, for fear of all the lurking dangers and threatening disasters.

Take my own case. In the hopeful 1950s I found it quite daring and paradoxical enough to advocate a growth pattern corresponding to figure 1. I just *had* to repress the thought that the process depicted there implies to some extent the antagonistic process shown in figure 2. Twenty-five years later we have learned so much, alas, about the enormous difficulties and tensions that come with any social change that the antagonistic growth process portrayed in figure 2 no longer looks so gratuitously harrowing as it would have earlier. In fact, I now want to argue that the process of antagonistic unbalanced growth—it could be called "sailing against the wind"—is far more common than one might think.

---

[31]Reprinted in *Trespassing*.

[32]For an early critique of this sort, see Warren F. Ilchman and R. C. Bargave, "Balanced Thought and Economic Growth," *Economic Development and Cultural Change,* July 1966: 385–99.

In figure 2 we are free to make the two coordinates represent not the incomes of two important social groups, such as workers and capitalists, but more generally two important social objectives such as economic stability (internal and external) and growth, or growth and equity (a less unequal distribution of income and wealth), or, for that matter, equity and stability. As soon as we do so we realize that sailing against the wind is actually how Western societies have frequently been traveling when they were moving forward at all.

I have two reasons to suggest. First, each of these objectives is so difficult to achieve that progress with just one of them requires the utmost concentration of intellectual energies and political resources. The result is neglect of other crucial objectives, a neglect that subsequently comes to public attention; the resulting criticism then leads to a change in course, to a new concentration—and a new neglect.

Second, the sailing-against-the-wind pattern is congenial to the democratic form of government, and particularly to the two-party system of democratic governance. If, in such a system, each of the two parties retains a characteristic physiognomy or ideological consistency of its own, then each party will give very distinct priorities to such social objectives as growth, equity, and stability; with the parties alternating in power, society is likely to move, in the best of circumstances, as though it were sailing against the wind.[33]

It does seem, at first blush, an odd and even perverse way of moving forward—a course in which some important social group is constantly aggrieved and attacked and some primary social objective constantly disregarded and even set back. Yet this may be the characteristic, even the only available pattern, of progress in a society which lives by the canons of competitive politics. Such a society is necessarily divided into "ins" and "outs," with the interests and aspirations of the latter being neglected until it

[33]An empirical study and verification for twelve Western European and North American nations during the postwar period is in Douglas A. Hibbs, Jr., "Political Parties and Macro Economic Policy," *American Political Science Review*, December 1977: 1467–87.

is their turn to take over and to turn the tables on their opponents.

In sum, the art of moving society forward in a democracy is to do so in spite of substantial and justified discontent on the part of some important groups, followed by similar discontent on the part of others. At any one point in time, there is always not only strife and clash and conflict, but also loss of some valuable terrain previously gained. Yet it is possible that all-around progress is being achieved behind the back, so to speak, of the parties and groups in conflict. Democracy is consolidated when, after a few alternations of the parties in power, the various groups come to realize that, strangely enough, they have all gained.

There can of course be no certainty that the antagonistic moves here described will actually have this happy outcome. They can just as well do the opposite—in figure 2 the movement would simply have to be visualized as taking place in the direction opposite to that of the optimistic arrow there shown. In such circumstances democracy will be proclaimed to be in crisis and to be involved in playing zero- or negative-sum games. "Fundamental" solutions will now be sought, such as an end to the "destructive" party struggle and a national accord on basic objectives, so that society can move forward along a "balanced" path with simultaneous progress being made toward each and every one of the agreed-upon objectives. Such is the ever present corporatist and authoritarian temptation that arises when a pluralist regime puts in a poor performance. Our antagonistic, sailing-against-the-wind growth pattern makes it clear that another solution might also be available, one that has the considerable merit of not jettisoning the pattern of competitive politics.

By now my self-criticism of unbalanced growth has obviously taken a strange turn. I started by faulting myself for not having recognized, in the course of my advocacy of unbalanced growth, that such growth could imply for a while an actual decline in the incomes of the initially nonexpanding sector. But then I established a connection between this antagonistic growth model and the awkward way in which a democracy typically moves forward. Thus my self-blame soon ran out of steam, and I ended up presenting this growth model as a remarkable social invention by means of which pluralist politics and the achievement of multiple social objectives can be reconciled.

What I have done, once again, is to show that my original unbalanced growth model, intended exclusively for the better comprehension of processes in developing countries, has its uses, after a slight transformation, in dealing with problems of political economy in the advanced countries. And this demonstration gives me considerable satisfaction: in the end, the advanced countries too are forced into awkward solutions to their problems, they too do things seemingly *al revés*, the wrong way around!

CONCLUSION

The organizers of this symposium recommended—though not in these exact terms—that we should both celebrate and criticize our ideas of yesteryear in the light of intervening events and experiences. Like my distinguished fellow pioneers, I have found it difficult to be evenhanded in this dual task. Moreover, what started out here and there as a confession of sins tended to end up, curiously enough, as a confession of faith.

It is probably a futile exercise to go back to a work, some twenty-five years later, and to pronounce some ideas as still good, others as disproven; some as having had a wholesome influence, others as having been harmful—and then to strike a balance with a bottom line. It makes more sense to attempt what Benedetto Croce pointed to with one of his titles that read *What Is Alive and What Is Dead in Hegel's Philosophy*, that is, to evaluate what is alive and what is dead of our work. There too, of course, the authors themselves are poor judges, and all they can do is to try to convince the reader that there is quite some life left in those old "written and painted thoughts" and that they continue to evolve in interesting ways.

One last remark, on the impact of new ideas. Since my thoughts on development were largely dissents, critical of both old and new orthodoxies, they have led to lively debates, thus helping, together with the contributions of others, to make the new field of development economics attractive and exciting, back in the 1950s and 1960s. I rather think that this was the major positive contribution of my work as well as its principal impact.

Perhaps there is a general point here. The effect of new theories and ideas is much less direct than we often think: to a considerable extent, it comes by way of the general impetus that is given to a certain field of studies. As a result of a few contributions, that field suddenly comes alive with discussion and controversy and attracts some of the more intelligent, energetic, and dedicated members of a generation. This is the indirect, or *recruitment*, effect of new ideas, as opposed to their direct, or *persuasion*, effect, which is usually the only one to be considered. It happens frequently that the recruitment effect is far more significant and durable than the persuasion effect. The importance of the recruitment effect explains, among other things, why the influence of new ideas is so unpredictable and why it is so difficult—and often ludicrous—to assign intellectual responsibility for actual policy decisions, let alone for policy outcomes.

The field of development studies is a remarkable case in point. After the success of the Marshall Plan, the underdevelopment of Asia, Africa, and Latin America loomed as the major unresolved economic problem on any "Agenda for a Better World." At the same time, various contending views came forward on how best to tackle that problem. The recruitment effect of this combination of circumstances was notable. As the problem turned out to be tougher and more hydra-headed than any of us had anticipated, this was most fortunate. In this manner, we, the so-called pioneers, can take pride, not in having solved the problems of development, but in having contributed to attracting into our field a large number of people who will carry on.

2. The Concept of Interest:
FROM EUPHEMISM
TO TAUTOLOGY

"Interest" or "interests" is one of the most central and controversial concepts in economics and, more generally, in social science and history. It is also extremely versatile, not to say ambiguous, and its meaning has been shifting a great deal. Since coming into widespread use, in various European countries around the latter part of the sixteenth century as essentially the same Latin-derived word (*intérêt, interesse,* etc.), the concept has stood for the fundamental forces, based on the drive for self-preservation and self-aggrandizement, that motivate or should motivate the actions of the prince or the state, of the individual, and, later, of groups of people occupying a similar social or economic position (classes, interest groups). When related to the individual, the concept has at times had a very inclusive meaning, encompassing interest in honor, glory, self-respect, and even afterlife, while, at other times, it became wholly confined to the drive for economic advantage. Correspondingly, "pursuing one's interests" can cover—to the point of tautology—all of human action while it will more usefully designate a specific manner or *style* of conduct, known variously as "rational" or as "instrumental" action.

The esteem in which interest-motivated behavior is held has also varied drastically. The term was originally pressed into service as a euphemism serving, already in the late Middle Ages, to make respectable an activity, the taking of interest on loans, that had long been considered contrary to divine law and known as the sin of usury. In its wide meanings, the term achieved at times enormous presitge as key to a workable, peaceful, and progressive social order. But it has also been attacked as degrading to the human spirit and as dangerously disruptive and corrosive of the foundations of society. An inquiry into these multiple meanings and appreciations is in effect an exploration of much of economic history and in particular of the history of economic and political doctrine in the West over the past four centuries.

Moreover, the concept is still central in contemporary economics and political economy: the construct of the self-interested, isolated individual who chooses freely and rationally between alternative courses of action after computing their prospective costs and benefits to him- or herself, that is, while ignoring costs and benefits to other people and to society at large, underlies much of welfare economics; and the same perspective has yielded important, if disturbing, contributions to a broader science of social interactions, showing how the unfettered pursuit of private interest can lead to inefficient and harmful outcomes: examples are the decision problem known as the Prisoner's Dilemma, the obstacles to collective action because of free riding, and the problems of ensuring an adequate supply of public goods in general.

Two essential elements appear to characterize interest-propelled action: *self-centeredness,* that is, predominant attention of the actor to the consequences of any contemplated action for himself; and *rational calculation,* that is, a systematic attempt at evaluating prospective costs, benefits, satisfactions, and the like. Calculation could be considered the dominant or fundamental element: once action is supposed to be informed only by careful estimation of costs and benefits, with most weight necessarily being given to those that are better known and more quantifiable, it tends to become self-referential by virtue of the simple fact that each person is best informed about his or her *own* desires, satisfactions, disappointments, and sufferings.

INTEREST AND STATECRAFT

Rational calculation was also preponderant in the emergence of the concept of interest-motivated action on the part of the prince in the sixteenth and seventeenth centuries. Self-centeredness was then either hidden from view, as the interest of the prince was assumed to be identical with that of his subjects, or treated as a matter of course, rather than of choice; in relation to other princes, the absence of interests in common and the hazards of antagonistic coexistence were considered to be unalterable facts of nature.

It was probably this stress on rational calculation that accounts for the high marks that interest (interest-governed behavior) received during the late sixteenth- and early seventeenth-century phases of its career in politics. The term actually did duty on two fronts. First, it permitted the emergent science of statecraft to assimilate the important insights of Machiavelli. The author of *The Prince* had almost strained to advertise those aspects of politics that clashed with conventional morality. He dwelt on instances where the prince was well-advised or even duty-bound to practice cruelty, mendacity, treason, and so on. Just as, in connection with money lending, the term interest came into use as a euphemism for the earlier term usury, so did it impose itself on the political vocabulary as a means of anesthetizing, assimilating, and developing some of Machiavelli's shocking insights. "Reason of state" was another such term, which as Meinecke later showed explicitly referred to the new practical rationality that came into favor.

But in the early modern age, "interest" was not only a label under which a ruler was given new latitude or was absolved from feeling guilty about following a practice he had previously been taught to consider as immoral: the term also served to impose new restraints, as it enjoined the prince to pursue his interests with a rational, calculating spirit that would often imply prudence and moderation. At the beginning of the seventeenth century, the interests of the sovereign were contrasted with the wild and destructive passions, that is, with the immoderate and foolish seeking of glory and other excesses involved in pursuing the by then discredited heroic ideal of the Middle Ages and the Renaissance. This disciplinary aspect of the doctrine of interest was particularly driven home in the influential essay *On the Interest of Princes and States of Christendom* by the Huguenot statesman, the Duke of Rohan (1579–1638).

The interest doctrine thus served to release the ruler from certain traditional restraints (or guilt feelings) only to subject him to new ones that were felt to be far more efficacious than the well-worn appeals to religion, morals, or abstract reason. Genuine hope arose that, with princely or national interest as guide, statecraft would be able to produce a more stable political order and a more peaceful world. A distinct nineteenth-century echo of these seventeenth-century notions is heard in various pronouncements of Bismarck, and particularly in a famous foreign policy speech of 1888 where he contrasted legitimate *Interessenpolitik* with arrogant *Machtpolitik*, which he defined as a policy "that seeks to influence and press upon the policy of other countries and to call the tune *outside* of one's own sphere of interests.[1]

Interest and Individual Behavior

The early career of the interest concept with regard to statecraft finds a remarkable parallel in the role it played in shaping behavior codes for individual men and women in society. Here also a new license went hand in hand with a new restraint.

The new license consisted in the legitimation and even praise that was bestowed upon the single-minded pursuit of material wealth and upon activities conducive to its accumulation. Just as Machiavelli had opened up new horizons for the prince, so did Mandeville two centuries later lift a number of don'ts for the commoner, in this case primarily in relation to moneymaking. Once again, a new insight into human behavior or into the social order was first proclaimed as a startling, shocking paradox. Like Machiavelli, Mandeville presented his thesis on the beneficial

---

[1]Cited in Koselleck, p. 349.

effects on the general welfare of the luxury trades (which had long been strictly regulated) in the most scandalous possible fashion, by referring to the activities, drives, and emotions associated with these trades as "private vices." Here again, his essential message was eventually absorbed into the general stock of accepted practice by changing the language with which he had proclaimed his discovery. For the third time, euphemistic resort was had to "interest," this time in substitution for such terms as "avarice," "love of lucre," and so on. The transition from one set of terms to the other is nicely reflected by the first lines of David Hume's 1742 essay "On the Independency of Parliament":

> Political writers have established it as a maxim, that, in contriving any system of government and fixing the several checks and balances of the constitution, every man ought to be supposed a *knave,* and to have no other end, in all his actions, than private interest. By this interest we must govern him, and, by means of it, make him, notwithstanding his insatiable avarice and ambition, cooperate to public good.[2]

Here interest is explicitly equated with knavishness and "insatiable avarice." But soon thereafter the memory of these unsavory synonyms of interest was suppressed, as in Adam Smith's famous statement about the butcher, the brewer, and the baker who are driven to supply us with our daily necessities through their interest rather than their benevolence. Smith thus did for Mandeville what the Duke of Rohan had done for Machiavelli. His doctrine of the Invisible Hand, which held that the general welfare is best served by everyone catering to his private interests, legitimated total absorption of the citizens in their own affairs and thereby served to assuage any guilt feelings that might have been harbored by the many Englishmen who were drawn into commerce and industry during the eighteenth century but had been brought up under the civic humanist code enjoining them to serve the public interest *directly.* They were now reassured that by pursuing their private gain they were doing so *indirectly.*

---

[2]See Hume, pp. 117–18.

In fact, Adam Smith was not content to praise the pursuit of private gain. Prefiguring Milton Friedman's hostility to corporations contributing funds to charities and community improvements, he berated citizens' involvement in public affairs, by adding that he had "never known much good done by those who affected to trade for the public good." This may be just one of Smith's ill-humored sideswipes, but ten years before Sir James Steuart, in his *Inquiry into the Principles of Political Oeconomy*, had supplied an interesting explanation for a similar aversion toward citizens' involvement in public affairs:

> ... were everyone to act for the public, and neglect himself, the statesman would be bewildered ... were a people to become quite disinterested, there would be no possibility of governing them. Everyone might consider the interest of his country in a different light, and many might join in the ruin of it, by endeavoring to promote its advantages.[3]

In counterpart to the new area of authorized and recommended behavior, these statements point to the important restraints that accompanied the doctrine of interest. For the individual citizen or subject as for the ruler, interest-propelled action meant originally action informed by rational calculation in any area of human activity—political, cultural, economic, personal, and so on. In the seventeenth century and through part of the eighteenth, this sort of methodical, prudential, interest-guided action was seen as vastly preferable to actions dictated by the violent and unruly passions—the French liked to speak about *la violence et le désordre des passions*. Hope was held out that the steady, if self-centered, pull of the interests might serve more efficiently as a brake on passionate behavior than the traditional appeals to reason, duty, morals, and religion. At the same time, the interests of the vast majority of people, that is, of those outside of the highest reaches of power, came to be more narrowly defined as economic, material, or "moneyed" interests, probably because the non-elite was deemed to busy itself primarily with scrounging a

---

[3]See Steuart, pp. 243–44.

living with no time left to worry about honor, glory, and the like. In this manner, the infatuation with interest helped to bestow legitimacy and prestige on commercial and related private activities that had hitherto ranked rather low in public esteem; correspondingly, the Renaissance ideal of glory, with its implicit celebration of the public sphere, was downgraded and debunked as a mere exercise in the destructive passion of self-love.[4]

Adam Smith and Sir James Steuart echo this feeling of mistrust toward, and disaffection from, activities that are aimed at achieving the public good directly. This change in attitude toward public involvement may have reflected a general mood: it is perhaps significant that only in the course of the eighteenth century did the verb "to meddle" firmly acquire its present-day derogatory sense.[5] The meaning of the French *se mêler de* has had a similar evolution. Previously these terms had a neutral and sometimes even a positive connotation: after all, to meddle is to care for somebody or something outside of one's own immediate circle or area of interest, an attitude and activity that became offensive only in an era when to mind one's own business had become enthroned as a general rule of conduct.

THE POLITICAL BENEFITS OF AN INTEREST-BASED SOCIAL ORDER

The idea that the interests, understood as the methodical pursuit and accumulation of private wealth, would bring a number of benefits in the political realm took various distinct forms. There was, first of all, the expectation that they would achieve at the macrolevel what they were supposed to accomplish for the individual: hold back the violent passions of the "rulers of mankind." Here the best known proposition, voiced early in the eighteenth century, says that the expansion of commerce is

---

[4]See my *The Passions and the Interests*, pp. 31–42.
[5]I owe this to a personal communication from Quentin Skinner.

incompatible with the use of force in international relations and would gradually make for a peaceful world. Still more utopian—and therefore perhaps half-forgotten—hopes were held out for the effects of commerce on domestic politics: the web of interests delicately woven by thousands of transactions would make it impossible for the sovereign to interpose his power brutally and wantonly through what was called "grands coups d'autorité" by Montesquieu or "the folly of despotism" by Sir James Steuart. This thought was carried further in the early nineteenth century when the intricacies of expanding industrial production compounded those of commerce: in the technocratic vision of Saint-Simon the time was at hand when economic exigencies would put an end, not just to *abuses* of the power of the state, but to any power whatsover of man over man: politics would be replaced by administration of "things." As is well known this conjecture was taken up by Marxism with its prediction of the withering away of the state under communism. In this manner, an argument that a century earlier had been advanced on behalf of emergent capitalism was refurbished for a new, *anti*capitalist utopia.

Another line of thought about the political effects of an interest-driven society looks less at the disciplines and constraints such a society will impose upon those who govern than at the difficulties of the task of governing. As already noted, a world where people methodically pursue their private interests was believed to be far more predictable, and hence *more governable*, than one where the citizens are vying with each other for honor and glory. There was thought to be a huge common gain here, quite apart from the proposition that voluntary acts of exchange necessarily imply the existence of mutual benefits.

The stability and lack of turbulence that were expected to characterize a country where men pursue single-mindedly their material interests were very much on the minds of some of the "inventors" of America, such as James Madison and Alexander Hamilton. The enormous prestige and influence of the interest concept at the time of the founding of America is well expressed in Hamilton's statement: "The safest reliance of every government is on man's interests. This is a principle of human nature, on which all political speculation, to be just, must be founded."[6]

Finally, at the most naive level, a number of writers essentially extrapolated from the putative personality traits of the individual trader, as the prototype of interest-driven man, to the general characteristics of a society where traders would predominate. In the eighteenth century, perhaps as a result of some continuing, if unavowed, disdain for economic pursuits, commerce and moneymaking were often described as essentially innocuous or "innocent" pastimes, in contrast no doubt with the more violent or more strenuous ways of the upper or lower classes. Commerce was to bring "gentle" and "polished" manners. In French, the term innocent appended to commerce was often coupled with *doux* (sweet, gentle), or *adoucir* (soften, render gentle), and what has been called the thesis of the *doux commerce* held that commerce was a powerful civilizing agent diffusing prudence, probity, and similar virtues within and among trading societies. Only under the impact of the French Revolution did some doubt arise on the direction of the causal link between commerce and civilized society: taken aback by the outbreak of social violence on a large scale, Edmund Burke suggested that the expansion of commerce depended itself on the *prior* existence of "manners" and "civilization" and on what he called "natural protecting principles" grounded in "the spirit of a gentleman" and "the spirit of religion."[7]

It was inevitable that the celebration of the interests should have enhanced the esteem accorded to those social groups that were primarily involved in commerce and industry. An early expression of this tendency is in *Robinson Crusoe* where Crusoe's father explains to his son—to dissuade him from his plans—that the "middle state" is "the most suited to human happiness, not exposed to the miseries and hardships, the labour and sufferings of the mechanic part of mankind, and not embarrassed with the pride, luxury, ambition and envy of the upper part of mankind."

Similar expressions of admiration for what was later often

---

[6]Cited in Ball, p. 45.
[7]Cited by Pocock.

called the "middling rank of men" or simply "middle ranks" (rather than middle class) can be found in the writings of David Hume, Adam Smith, Adam Ferguson, and of the other exponents of the Scottish Enlightenment. In the nineteenth century James Mill waxed remarkably eloquent on this subject.[8] In France, the praise of the bourgeoisie as such was never quite so unreserved, but some of its constituent parts, such as the commercial community, rose in prestige as a result of the praise for the *doux commerce*.

THE INVISIBLE HAND

The capstone of the doctrine of self-interest was of course Adam Smith's Invisible Hand. Even though this doctrine, being limited to the economic domain, was more modest than the earlier speculations on the beneficent *political* effects of trade and exchange, it soon came to dominate the discussion. An intriguing paradox was involved in stating that the *general* interest and welfare would be promoted by the self-interested activities of numerous decentralized operators. To be sure, this was not the first nor the last time that such a claim of identity or coincidence or harmony of interests of a part with those of a whole has been put forward. Hobbes had advocated an absolute monarchy on the ground that this form of government brings about an identity of interests between ruler and ruled; as just noted, the writers of the Scottish Enlightenment saw an identity of interest between the general interests of British society and the interests of the middle ranks; such an identity between the interests of one class and those of society later became a cornerstone of Marxism, with the middling ranks having of course been supplanted by the proletariat; and finally, the American pluralist school in political science returned essentially to the Smithian scheme of harmony between many self-interests and the general interest, with Smith's individual economic operators having been replaced by contending "interest groups" on the political stage.

---

[8]See Collini, Winch and Burrow, p. 122.

All these *Harmonielehren* (and I have probably been omitting some) have two factors in common: the "realistic" affirmation that we have to deal with men and women, or with groups thereof, "as they really are"; and an attempt to prove that it is possible to achieve a workable and progressive social order with these highly imperfect subjects, and, as it were, behind their backs. The mixture of paradoxical insight and alchemy involved in these constructs makes them powerfully attractive, but also accounts for their ultimate vulnerability. Perhaps social scientists ought to be advised to use caution in the construction of any further harmony-of-interests doctrines.

THE INTERESTS ATTACKED

The infatuation of the seventeenth and eighteenth centuries with the new insights offered by the concept of interest was remarkable. From the seventeenth-century English proverbs "Interest will not lie" or "Interest governs the world" to the late eighteenth-century dictum of the French *philosophe* Helvétius, "As the physical world is ruled by the laws of movement so is the moral universe ruled by the laws of interest," and to Hamilton's already noted similar pronouncement, interest was perceived as the key that unlocks the secrets of the social universe.

The seventeenth century was perhaps the real heyday of the interest doctrine. Governance of the social world by interest was then viewed as an alternative to the rule of destructive passions; that was surely a lesser evil, and possibly an outright blessing. In the eighteenth century, the doctrine received a substantial boost in the economic domain through the doctrine of the Invisible Hand, but it was indirectly weakened by the emergence of a more optimistic view of the passions: such passionate sentiments and emotions as curiosity, generosity, and sympathy were then given detailed attention, the latter in fact by Adam Smith himself in his *Theory of Moral Sentiments*. In comparison to such fine, newly discovered or rehabilitated springs of human action, interest no longer looked nearly so attractive. Here was one reason for the reaction against the interest paradigm that unfolded toward the end of the eighteenth century and was to fuel several powerful nineteenth-century intellectual movements, starting with romanticism.

Actually the passions did not have to be wholly transformed into benign sentiments to be thought respectable and even admirable by a new generation. Once the interests appeared to be truly in command with the vigorous commercial and industrial expansion of the age, a general lament went up for "the world we have lost." The French Revolution brought another sense of loss and Edmund Burke joined the two when he exclaimed, in his *Reflections on the Revolution in France,* "the age of chivalry is gone; that of sophisters, oeconomists and calculators has succeeded; and the glory of Europe is extinguished forever." This famous statement came a bare fourteen years after the *Wealth of Nations* had denounced the rule of the "great lords" as a "scene of violence, rapine and disorder" and had celebrated the benefits flowing from everyone catering to his interests through orderly economic pursuits. Now Burke was an intense admirer of Adam Smith and took much pride in the identity of views on economic matters between himself and Smith. His "age of chivalry" statement, so contrary to the intellectual legacy of Smith, therefore signals one of those sudden changes in the general mood and understanding from one age to the next of which the exponents themselves are hardly aware. Burke's lament set the tone for much of the subsequent romantic protest against an order based on the interests which, once it appeared to be dominant, was seen by many as lacking nobility, mystery, and beauty.

This nostalgic reaction merged with the observation that the interests, that is, the drive for material wealth, were not nearly so "innocuous," "innocent," or "mild" as had been thought or advertised. To the contrary, it was now the drive for material advantage that suddenly loomed as a subversive force of enormous power. Thomas Carlyle thought that all traditional values were threatened by "that brutish god-forgetting Profit-and-Loss Philosophy" and protested that "cash payment is not the only nexus of man with man."[9] The phrase "cash nexus" was taken over by Marx and Engels, who used it to good effect in the first section of the *Communist Manifesto* where they painted a lurid picture of the moral and cultural havoc wrought by the conquering bourgeoisie.

In the same vein Proudhon saw property as a boundless revolutionary force. Trying to snatch good from evil, he conceived of the modern idea that the power of property might serve to check the equally terrifying power of the state: human liberty would be founded on this tension.[10] But such constructive or optimistic thoughts were exceedingly rare. Among the critics of capitalist society the accent was in general on the destructiveness of the new energies that were released by a social order in which the interests were given free rein. In fact, the thought arose that these forces were so wild and out of control that they might undermine the very foundations on which the social order was resting, that they were thus bent on self-destruction. In a startling reversal, feudal society, which had earlier been treated as "rude and barbarous" and was thought to be in permanent danger of dissolution because of the unchecked passions of violent rulers and grandees, was perceived in retrospect to have nurtured such values as honor, respect, friendship, trust, and loyalty, that were essential for the functioning of an interest-dominated order, but were relentlessly, if inadvertently, undermined by it. This argument was already contained in part in Burke's assertion that it is civilized society that lays the groundwork for commerce rather than vice versa; it was elaborated by a large and diverse group of authors, from Richard Wagner via Schumpeter to Karl Polanyi and Fred Hirsch.[11]

---

[9]*Past and Present*, p. 187.
[10]See my *The Passions and the Interests*, p. 120.
[11]See chapter 5, pp. 105–139.

THE INTERESTS DILUTED

While the interest doctrine thus met with considerable opposition and criticism in the nineteenth century, its prestige remained nevertheless high, particularly because of the vigorous development of economics as a new body of scientific thought. Indeed, the success of this new science made for attempts to utilize its insights, such as the interest concept, for elucidating some noneconomic aspects of the social world. In his "Essay on Government" (1820), James Mill formulated the first "economic" theory of politics and based it—just as was later done by Schumpeter, Anthony Downs, Mancur Olson, and others—on the assumption of rational self-interest. But this widening of the use of the concept turned out to be something of a disservice. In politics, so Mill had to recognize, the gap between the "real" interest of the citizen and "a false supposition [i.e., perception] of interest" can be extremely wide and problematic. This difficulty provided an opening for Macaulay's withering attack in the *Edinburgh Review* (1829). Macaulay pointed out that Mill's theory was empty: interest "means only that men, if they can, will do as they choose . . . it is . . . idle to attribute any importance to a proposition which, when interpreted, means only that a man had rather do what he had rather do."

The charge that the interest doctrine was essentially tautological acquired greater force as more parties climbed on the bandwagon of interest, attempting to bend the concept to their own ends. Like so many key concepts used in everyday discourse, "interest" had never been strictly defined. While individual self-interest in material gain predominated, broader meanings were never completely lost sight of, as appears from the expression "narrow" self-interest, which is presumably distinguished from another kind of self-interest. An extremely inclusive interpretation of the concept was put forward at a very early stage of its history: Pascal's Wager—his demonstration that it is "rational" to act as though God existed, in the absence of certain knowledge about the matter—was nothing but an attempt to demonstrate that belief in God (hence, conduct in accordance with His precepts) was strictly in our (long-term) self-interest. Thus the concepts of *enlightened self-interest* or *intérêt bien compris* have a long history. But they received a boost and special, concrete meaning in the course of the nineteenth century. With the contemporary revolutionary outbreaks and movements as an ominous backdrop, advocates of social reform were able to argue that a dominant social group is well advised to surrender some of its privileges or to improve the plight of the lower classes so as to ensure social peace ("give up something not to lose everything"). "Enlightened" self-interest of the upper classes and conservative opinion was appealed to, for example, by the French and English advocates of universal suffrage or electoral reform at mid-century (the introduction of universal manhood suffrage in France after the 1848 Revolution was expected to "close the era of revolutions");[12] it was similarly invoked by the promoters of the early social-welfare legislation in Germany and elsewhere toward the end of the century, and again by Keynes and the Keynesians who favored limited intervention of the state in the economy through countercyclical policy and "automatic stabilizers" resulting from welfare-state provisions. These appeals were often made by reformers who, while fully convinced of the intrinsic value and social justice of the measures they advocated, attempted to enlist the support of important groups by appealing to their "longerterm" rather than short-term and therefore presumably *shortsighted* interests. But the advocacy was not only tactical. It was sincerely put forward and testified to the continued prestige of the notion that interest-motivated social behavior was the best guarantee of a stable and harmonious social order.

Whereas enlightened self-interest was something the upper classes of society were in this manner pressed to ferret out and to pursue, the lower classes were similarly exhorted, at about the same epoch but from different quarters, to raise their sights above day-to-day interests and pursuits. Marx and the Marxists invited the working class to become aware of its *real interests* and to shed the "false consciousness" from which it was said to be suf-

---

[12]See my *Shifting Involvements*, pp. 112–117.

fering as long as it did not throw itself wholeheartedly into the class struggle. Once again, the language of interests was borrowed for the purpose of characterizing and signifying a type of behavior a group was being pressed to follow.

Here, then, was one way in which the concept of interest-motivated behavior came to be diluted. Another was the progressive loss of the sharp distinction an earlier age had made between the passions and the interests. Already Adam Smith had used the two concepts jointly and interchangeably. Even though it became abundantly clear in the nineteenth century that the desire to accumulate wealth was anything but the "calm passion" as which it had been categorized and commended by some eighteenth-century philosophers, there was no return to the earlier distinction between the interests and the passions or between the wild and the mild passions. Perhaps this was so because moneymaking had once and for all been identified with the concept of interest so that all forms of this activity, however passionate or irrational, were automatically thought of as interest-motivated. As striking new forms of accumulation and industrial or financial empire-building made their appearance, new concepts were introduced, such as Schumpeter's entrepreneurial leadership and intuition or Keynes's "animal spirits" (of the capitalists.) But they were not contrasted with the interests, and were rather assumed to be one of their manifestations.

In this manner the interests came to cover virtually the entire range of human actions, from the narrowly self-centered to the sacrificially altruistic, and from the prudently calculated to the passionately compulsive. In the end, interest stood behind anything people do or wish to do, and to explain human action by interest thus did turn into the vacuous tautology denounced by Macaulay. It so happened that, at about the same time, other key and time-honored concepts of economic analysis, such as utility and value, became similarly drained of their earlier psychological or normative content. The positivistically oriented science of economics that flourished during much of this century felt it could do without any of these terms and replaced them by the less value- or psychology-laden "revealed preference" and "maximizing under constraints." And thus it came to pass that interest, which had rendered such long, faithful, and multiple services as a euphemism (for usury, for cruelty and other types of amoral princely behavior, and for avarice and love of lucre), was now superseded by various even more neutral and colorless neologisms.

It may be conjectured that the development of the self-interest concept and of economic analysis in general in the direction of positivism and formalism was related to the discovery, toward the end of the nineteenth century, of the instinctual-intuitive, the habitual, the unconscious, the ideologically and neurotically driven—in short, to the extraordinary vogue for the nonrational that characterized virtually all of the influential philosophical, psychological, and sociological thinking of the age. It was out of the question for economics, all based on rationally pursued self-interest, to incorporate the new findings into its own apparatus. So that discipline reacted to the contemporary intellectual temper by withdrawing from psychology to the greatest possible extent, by emptying its basic concepts of their psychological origin—a survival strategy that turned out to be highly successful. It is of course difficult to prove that the rise of the nonrational in psychology and sociology and the triumph of positivism and formalism in economics were truly connected in this way. Some evidence is supplied by the remarkable case of Pareto: he made fundamental, *interrelated* contributions both to a sociology that stressed the complex "nonlogical" (as he put it) aspects of social action and to an economics that is emancipated from dependence on psychological hedonism.

CURRENT TRENDS

Lately there have been signs of discontent with the progressive evisceration of the concept of interest. On the conservative side, there was a return to the orthodox meaning of interest and the doctrine of enlightened self-interest was impugned. Apart from the discovery, first made by Tocqueville, that reform is just as likely to unleash as to prevent revolution, it was pointed out that most well-meant reform moves and regulations have "perverse" side effects which compound rather than alleviate the social ills one had set out to cure. It was best, so it appeared, not to stray from the narrow path of narrow self-interest, and it was confusing and pointless to dilute this concept.

Others agreed with the latter judgment, but for different reasons and with different conclusions. They also disliked the maneuver of having every kind of human action masquerade under the interest label. But they regarded as relevant for economics certain human actions and activities which cannot be accounted for by the traditional notion of self-interest: actions motivated by altruism, by commitment to ethical values, by concern for the group and the public interest, and, perhaps most important, the varieties of noninstrumental behavior. A beginning has been made by various economists and other social scientists to take these kinds of activities and behavior seriously, that is, to abandon the attempt to categorize them as mere variants of interest-motivated activity.[13]

One important aspect of these various forms of behavior which do not correspond to the classical concept of interest-motivated action is that they are subject to considerable variation. Take actions in the public interest as an example. There is a wide range of such actions, from total involvement in some protest movement down to voting on Election Day and further down to mere grumbling about, or just commenting on, some public policy within a small circle of friends or family—what Guillermo O'Donnell has called "horizontal voice" in contrast to the "vertical" voice directly addressed to the authorities. The actual degree of participation under more or less normal political conditions is subject to constant fluctuations along this continuum, in line with changes in economic conditions, government performance, personal development, and many other factors. As a result, with

---

[13]Among many other works, reference should be made to writings (cited in the Bibliographical References) by Boulding, Collard, Margolis, McPherson, Phelps, Pizzorno, Schelling, and Sen; see also chapter 6.

total time for private *and* public activity being limited, the intensity of citizens' dedication to their private affairs is also subject to constant change. Near-total privatization occurs only under certain authoritarian governments, for, as Benjamin Constant acutely noted, "the art of oppressive government is to keep all its citizens separated from each other."[14] The most repressive regimes not only do away with the free vote and any open manifestation of dissent, but also manage to suppress, through their display of terrorist power, all *private* expressions of inconformity with public policy, that is, all those manifestations of "horizontal voice" that are actually important forms of public involvement.

An arresting conclusion follows. That vaunted ideal of predictability, that alleged idyll of a privatized citizenry paying busy and exclusive attention to its economic interests and thereby serving the public interest indirectly, but never directly, becomes a reality only under wholly nightmarish political conditions! More civilized political circumstances necessarily imply a less transparent and less predictable society.

Actually, this outcome of the current inquiries into activities not strictly motivated by traditional self-interest is all to the good: for the only certain and predictable feature of human affairs is their unpredictability and the futility of trying to reduce human action to a single motive—such as interest.

Bibliographical References

Ball, Terence. "The Ontological Presuppositions and Political Consequences of a Social Science." In *Changing Social Science,* edited by D. R. Sabia, Jr., and J. T. Wallulis. Albany: State University of New York Press, 1983.

Boulding, Kenneth E. *The Economy of Love and Fear: A Preface to Grant Economics.* Belmont, Calif.: Wadsworth, 1973.

Burke, Edmund. *Reflections on the Revolution in France.* 1790.

Carlyle, Thomas. *Past and Present.* 1843. New York: New York University Press, 1977.

Collard, David. *Altruism and Economy: A Study in Non-selfish Economics.* Oxford: Robertson, 1978.

Collini, Stefan; Winch, Donald; and Burrow, John. *That Noble Science of Politics:*

---

[14]Cited in Holmes, p. 247.

A Study in Nineteenth-Century Intellectual History. Cambridge: Cambridge University Press, 1983.

Constant, Benjamin. *Principes de Politique.* Edited by Etienne Hofmann. Geneva: Droz, 1980.

Defoe, Daniel. *Robinson Crusoe.* 1719.

Hamilton, Alexander. "Letters from Phocion." 1784. Number 1. In *The Works of Alexander Hamilton,* edited by John C. Hamilton, vol. 2, p. 322. New York: C. S. Francis, 1851.

Himmelfarb, Gertrude. *The Idea of Poverty: England in the Early Industrial Age.* New York: Knopf, 1984.

Hirschman, Albert O. *The Passions and the Interests: Political Arguments for Capitalism before Its Triumph.* Princeton, N.J.: Princeton University Press, 1977.

————. *Shifting Involvements: Private Interest and Public Action.* Princeton, N.J.: Princeton University Press, 1982.

Holmes, Stephen. *Benjamin Constant and the Making of Modern Liberalism.* New Haven, Conn.: Yale University Press, 1984.

Hume, David. *Essays Moral, Political and Literary.* 1742. Edited by T. H. Green and T. H. Grose. London: Longmans, 1898.

Keynes, John Maynard. *The General Theory of Employment Interest and Money.* London: Macmillan, 1936.

Koselleck, Reinhart. "Der Interessebegriff im Wandel des sozialen und politische Kontexts." In *Geschichtliche Grundbegriffe.* Stuttgart: Klett-Cotta, 1982, III, 344–62.

Macaulay, Thomas B. "Mill's Essay on Government." 1829. In *Utilitarian Logic and Politics,* edited by J. Lively and J. Rees. Oxford: Clarendon, 1978.

McPherson, Michael S. "Limits on Self-seeking: The Role of Morality in Economic Life." In *Neoclassical Political Economy,* edited b D. C. Colander, pp. 71–85. Cambridge, Mass.: Ballinger, 1984.

Margolis, Howard. *Selfishness, Altruism, and Rationality.* Cambridge: Cambridge University Press, 1982.

Meinecke, Friedrich. *Die Idee der Staatsräson in der neueren Geschichte.* Munich: Oldenburg, 1924.

Mill, James. "Essay on Government." 1820. In *Utilitarian Logic and Politics,* edited by J. Lively and J. Rees. Oxford: Clarendon, 1978.

O'Donnell, Guillermo. "On the Convergences of Hirschman's *Exit, Voice, and Loyalty* and *Shifting Involvements.*" In *Development, Democracy, and the Art of Trespassing: Essays in Honor of Albert O. Hirschman,* edited by A. Foxley et al. Notre Dame, Ind.: University of Notre Dame Press, 1986.

Phelps, Edmund S., ed. *Altruism, Morality and Economic Theory.* New York: Russell Sage Foundation, 1975.

Pizzorno, Alessandro. "Sulla razionalità della scelta democratica." *Stato e Mercato,* April 1983. English version in *Telos,* Spring 1985.

Pocock, John G. A. "The Political Economy of Burke's Analysis of the French Revolution." *Historical Journal,* June 1982.

Rohan, Henri, Duc de. *De l'interest des princes et estats de la chrestiente.* 1638.

Schelling, Thomas C. *Choice and Consequence.* Cambridge, Mass.: Harvard University Press, 1984.

Schumpeter, Joseph. *The Theory of Economic Development.* 1911. Cambridge, Mass.: Harvard University Press, 1951.

Sen, Amartya. "Rational Fools: A Critique of the Behavioral Foundations of Economic Theory." *Philosophy and Public Affairs,* Summer 1977.

Smith, Adam. *An Inquiry into the Nature and Causes of the Wealth of Nations.* 1776.

Steuart, Sir James. *Inquiry into the Principles of Political Oeconomy.* 1761. Edited by A. S. Skinner. Chicago: University of Chicago Press, 1966.

Winch, Donald. "The Burke-Smith Problem and Late Eighteenth-Century Political and Economic Thought." 1984. *Historical Journal,* March 1985.

3. Linkages in Economic Development

I originally defined a linkage (or linkage effect) as a characteristic, more or less compelling sequence of investment decisions occurring in the course of industrialization and, more generally, of economic development. In putting forward the concept in *The Strategy of Economic Development*, I implicitly criticized the then dominant Harrod-Domar growth model in which growth depends only on the capital-output ratio and on the availability of capital as determined by the propensity to save and the inflow of capital from abroad. More generally, the concept arose from a perspective contesting the conventional representation of an economy where natural resources, factors of production, and entrepreneurship are all unequivocally available in given, if scarce, amounts and need only be efficiently allocated to various activities for best results. Instead I contended that "development depends not so much on finding optimal combinations for given resources and factors of production as on calling forth and enlisting for development purposes resources and abilities that are hidden, scattered, or badly utilized." This view led me to search for various inducing and mobilizing mechanisms. The resulting "strategy of unbalanced growth" values investment decisions not only because of their immediate contribution to output, but because of the larger or smaller impulse such decisions are likely to impart to further investment, that is, because of their linkages. The strategy has important implications for investment planning: it proposes that dynamic considerations, based on the linkages, should be allowed to complement the criterion of static efficiency.

BACKWARD AND FORWARD LINKAGES

For countries undertaking to industrialize in the second half of the twentieth century, two sequences held promise for generating this sort of extra pressure toward investment. First, an existing industrial operation—relying initially on imports not only for its equipment and machinery, but also for many of its material inputs—would make for some pressure toward the domestic manufacture of these inputs and eventually would also provide a market for a domestic capital goods industry. This dynamic I called *backward linkage,* since the direction of the stimulus toward further investment flows from the finished article back to the semiprocessed or raw materials from which it is made or to the machines which help make it.

Another stimulus toward additional investment points in the other direction and I therefore called it *forward linkage:* the existence of a given product line A, which is a final demand good or is used as an input in line B, acts as stimulant to the establishment of another line C which can also use A as an input.

The stimuli toward further investment are rather different for backward and forward linkages. The pressures toward backward linkage investments arise in part from normal entrepreneurial behavior, given the newly available market for intermediate goods. But there may also be resistance against such investments on the part of established industrialists, who prefer to continue relying on imported inputs for price and quality reasons. At the same time, state policies often favor backward linkage investments (which hold out the promise of foreign-exchange savings and of a more "integrated" industrial structure) through the promise of tariff protection and through various preferential foreign-exchange and credit allocations, particularly in periods of foreign-exchange stringency. The pressures toward forward linkage investments come primarily from the efforts of existing producers to increase and diversify the market for their products. In contrast to backward linkage, official development policy is not likely to be much concerned with promoting them, but wholehearted support will come from existing domestic producers—that is, from those who produce inputs for the to-be-linked industries.

The linkage dynamic made it possible to visualize the industrialization process in terms of an input-output matrix, most of whose cells would be empty to start with, but would progressively fill up in large part because of backward and forward linkage effects. This close connection with Leontief's input-output model, which was being given its first practical applications through the computation of input-output tables for various national economies in the 1950s, contributed to its favorable reception and probably gave it a certain advantage over related attempts at describing the dynamic of industrialization, such as Rostow's "leading sector," Perroux's "propulsive industry," or Dahmén's "development block." On the other hand, this connection sometimes made for too mechanistic a concept of the linkage dynamic, which is strongly influenced, as just noted, by state policies and other institutional factors.[1]

The connection with the input-output model made it appear that measurement of backward and forward linkages would be easy, but this was largely an illusion. Input-output analysis is by nature synchronic, whereas linkage effects need time to unfold. In a country setting out to industrialize, existing input-output tables cannot reveal which additional industrial branches are likely to be *created* in the wake of industrial investment in a given product line. The input-output framework is even less suited to tracing backward linkage effects toward the machinery and equipment industries. Nevertheless, once a developing country has a fairly broad industrial base, so that the expansion of a given industry or the coming on stream of a new one leads primarily to the *expansion* rather than to the *creation* of other industries,

---

[1]See Raj, "Linkages in Industrialization and Development Strategy."

the measurement of linkage effects through statistical devices based on input-output tables becomes more meaningful.

The technical problems of measurement of backward and forward linkages have been widely debated.[2] The most elaborate attempt at measurement has been carried out by a group of economists at the Employment Program for Latin America of the International Labor Office (PREALC) in Santiago, Chile, whose primary interest was in the direct and indirect effects of investments in a given industry on *employment,* rather than on industrial expansion in terms of output.[3] Employment (as well as output) linkages, based on the backward linkage concept, were calculated for six Latin American countries (Mexico, Brazil, Chile, Colombia, Peru, Guatemala) with the help of available input-output tables for one or two years of the 1970s. One of the more interesting findings concerned the distinction between large and small firms. Since small firms are comparatively labor-intensive, investment is generally thought to be more employment creating when it is directed to them rather than to large-scale industry. This was indeed the case for the less industrialized countries included in the study. But for the more advanced Latin American countries with a broad industrial structure, the difference virtually disappeared: because of the interdependence among large and small firms, an expansion of large-scale industry created as much employment—once the linkages, that is, indirect effects, are taken into account—as investment in small-scale industry. This counterintuitive result has implications for industrial and employment policy.

Given the difficulties of measurement, the linkage concept has been more influential as a general way of thinking about development strategy than as a precise, practical tool in project analysis or planning. In addition, it has contributed to the understanding of the growth process. It clarified the political economy of late industrialization and shed light on the earlier phase,

---

[2]See in particular *Quarterly Journal of Economics,* May 1976.
[3]See García and Marfán, *Estructuras industriales y eslabonamientos de empleo.*

during which the countries of the periphery were integrated into the world economy as exporters of primary products. I shall discuss these two areas of application in turn.

LINKAGES AND INDUSTRIALIZATION

The backward linkage dynamic is particularly important for the newly industrializing countries of the twentieth century because their industrialization has often started with the imparting of "last touches" to a host of imported inputs and then worked itself backward, in contrast to the process in the older industrial countries which of necessity had to proceed in a more "balanced" way, that is, with all industrial stages—finished, semiprocessed goods and machinery—being created more or less in tandem.[4] For the late industrializers of the twentieth century, vigorous pursuit of the backward linkage dynamic was therefore essential for achieving an industrial structure of any depth. Industrialization following this sequential, staged path became widely known as Import-Substituting Industrialization (ISI).

The centrality of backward linkage in the ISI process had important and somewhat contradictory social and political consequences. On the one hand, the original entrepreneurs of the process (those who started it through "last touches" industries) were often erstwhile importers who, in periods of foreign-exchange shortage, found it profitable to manufacture from imported inputs the finished articles they no longer could procure from abroad. Hence the importance of traders, frequently recent immigrants, and of foreign firms in the process and among the entrepreneurial groups. The often noted comparative weakness of the "national bourgeoisie" in the late industrializing countries may in this manner be related to the pattern of industrialization.

---

[4]See my "The Political Economy of Import-Substituting Industrialization in Latin America," *Quarterly Journal of Economics*, February 1968; reprinted in *A Bias for Hope*.

But the sequential unfolding of ISI was also responsible for a rather different characteristic: a good part of the newly emerging industrial establishment is likely to be tightly held by a few large-scale, vertically integrated family firms or "groups."[5] As long as industries were first established to occupy the last stage of manufacuring, with major inputs being imported, the firms operating in that stage would often be anxious, if only for reasons of quality control, to own the upstream factories that would be founded later to supply those inputs; and they would have the means to do so (with some help from financial institutions, of course) precisely because, between setting up one stage of manufacturing and the next, considerable time would elapse permitting accumulation of investible funds.

The resulting concentration of part of industrial production in a few vertically integrated "groups" sometimes coexists with the preeminent role played by immigrant minorities or foreigners. These two characteristic aspects of ISI have made for a third: in many countries the state promoted public enterprises that were meant to counteract or to preempt excessive domination over the industrial establishment either by foreigners and immigrants or by a few powerful private monopolistic groups.[6] Another reason for direct state intervention was that private industrialists frequently preferred to continue to rely on foreign suppliers of semi-processed and capital goods—this occasional resistance to backward linkage is yet another characteristic of ISI.

In the 1960s, the ISI process began to be faulted on two opposite counts: for running out of steam before accomplishing a great deal, and for being pushed to unreasonable and uneconomic lengths. Both critiques, originating of course in different camps, have sometimes been made simultaneously, with varying justifications. One group of critics posited an early stage of ISI, which was alleged to be "easy" in comparison to a later stage, when the easy stage is "exhausted" and further progress in pushing backward linkage—toward the more "basic" intermediate or

---

[5] See Leff.
[6] See Jones, ed., chapter 2.

capital-goods industries—runs into various obstacles: the size of the market is too small, the capital needed is too large to be raised locally, and the technology is controlled by transnational corporations. If these obstacles effectively stop further progress, industrialization is denounced as "stunted" and as "lacking integration"; alternatively, if it proceeds with foreign capital in key positions, industrialization, originally hailed as a harbinger of national emancipation, is viewed as bringing on a new "dependency," more insidious and debilitating than the earlier forms. Furthermore, O'Donnell suggested in 1975 that the problems of transition from the "easy" to the "difficult" stage of ISI bear some responsibility for the breakdown of democracy and the rise of authoritarian regimes in various Latin American countries during the 1960s and 1970s. Not much of this thesis, however, survived the animated debate to which it gave rise.[7]

A very different critique of an industrialization that has backward linkage as its principal engine emphasized the danger of doing too much rather than too little, because of the misallocation of resources the process was believed to entail. This neoclassical critique pointed out, for example, that, given the nature of the ISI process, the *effective* rate of protection granted to domestically produced finished articles was much higher than appeared from the nominal rates, because of the large proportion of the total value of these articles that was imported, usually at much lower or zero rates, as intermediate inputs.[8] While the proposition itself is correct, those high levels of effective protection are bound to decline once the intermediate inputs are in turn produced in the country and would hence be eligible for the level of protection generally available to domestically produced goods.[9] The more successful the process of backward linkage, the more likely it was, therefore, that excessive levels of effective protection, characteristic of the early stages of the process, would be brought down.

---

[7]See articles by Kaufman, Serra, and Hirschman in D. Collier, ed., *The New Authoritarianism in Latin America*.

[8]See Johnson.

[9]See Corden.

Customs duties were not the only element in the environment of protection that fostered the new import-substituting industries. An important sheltering device was unintended. In the years after World War II, a number of developing countries experienced inflation. In combination with fixed, hence lagging, exchange rates, the inflationary pressures resulted in long periods of currency overvaluation, which made it necessary to establish quantitative import controls. Such controls generally favored the new industries, with their high requirements of imported inputs and machinery, and the arrangement thus served to subsidize industrial investment and expansion. The subsidy was paid, via the overvalued exchange rate, by the exporters of traditional primary products. The resources that were transferred in this roundabout manner from the traditional agricultural or mining sectors to the emerging industrial establishment could not have been mobilized directly. In the industrializing societies of Latin America, for example, the interests tied to the traditional export sectors were still in a highly influential position, and it was out of the question to tax them outright.[10]

While ingenious in the short term, the usefulness of the arrangement was bound to decline with time. The discrimination against exports, resulting from the overvalued exchange rate, was not particularly serious during the first stages of industrial development, when most new manufacturers had their hands full asserting themselves in their own rapidly growing domestic market. Moreover, in the shorter run, export volume of some of the traditional products—tropical tree crops and minerals from existing installations—did not react adversely to the overvaluation. But conditions changed after a decade or two of the postwar industrialization drive. Exports of industrial products (as well as of a new generation of primary products—fish meal, soya, etc.) became possible in the conditions of rapidly expanding world trade characteristic of the sixties and early seventies. Because of scale economies, some linked industries could only be economically justified if export markets could be found for a portion of

---

[10]See Kafka, and Furtado.

their output almost from the start. Finally, the overvaluation interfered with the vigorous pursuit of the backward linkage dynamic itself as long as materials and machinery could be imported at bargain prices. It therefore became desirable to establish realistic exchange rates, to reduce the degree of protection, and to adopt a new set of policies for both continued industrialization and export promotion.

Such a correction of the course of economic policy was not easy to perform. On the one hand, it was resisted by groups that had prospered under the older set of policies. In some countries, such as Chile, on the other hand, the new course was imposed in the form of total reversal of previous policies as though they had been wholly misguided; in the process, considerable damage was caused to the industrial structure that had been built up and unemployment rose to very high levels.

CONSUMPTION LINKAGE

The linkage concept represented an attempt to identify specific powerful pressures toward investment decisions that make themselves felt in a growing economy. The forward and backward linkages are peculiarly direct pressures of that kind. Specially fashioned after observation of the industrialization process in the late developing countries, they were, not surprisingly, able to capture some of its distinctive features and problems, such as its sequential or staged character. Once formed, the linkage concept proved versatile: new types of linkage effects were identified and found useful for the analysis of a wide range of development experiences.

The mechanisms of the new linkages were more roundabout than the backward and forward variety. Thus *consumption linkage* is defined as the stimulus toward domestic production of consumer goods that will be undertaken as newly earned incomes are spent on such goods. In an open economy such goods will often be imported at first, but eventually domestic production will become an attractive proposition.

Consumption linkage is actually the *initial* step in the process of import-substituting industrialization. The backward and forward linkage dynamic can explain the *spread* of industrial activity from an established industrial nucleus, but how is it possible to account for a country's first generation of industrial plants? Many of these have typically come into being in the peripheral countries when increasing domestic incomes originating in export agriculture or mining caused imports of various consumer goods to reach a volume that made domestic manufacture economically attractive. Eventually some of these goods would be exported; as I put it, enjoying the paradox, the countries in question, "tend to develop a comparative advantage in the articles they *import*."[11] This whole process is far from smooth and gradual. Though basically connected with the growth of a country's primary exports, it often acquired special impetus when a period of trade expansion was followed by retrenchment due to world depression or international crisis: then, with demand for the imported articles well established and with imports temporarily unavailable, the incentives to domestic manufacture were strongest. These incentives were usually further buttressed by protective tariffs, at least in the noncolonial countries of the periphery.

Rising imports of consumer goods, such as textiles, into newly developing countries have often been blamed for the decay of local handicraft and artisanal production. It appears that they must be correspondingly credited with laying the groundwork for local industry, through consumption linkages.

The strength of consumption linkages and their effectiveness in inducing industrial development depend not only on the aggregate income stream to which primary exports give rise, but on many other factors, including the distribution of this income. The more egalitarian the distribution of a given income the larger will be the consumer demand for many typical products of modern industry and the more likely does it become that the domestic market will reach the size at which local production is warranted.

---

[11]See Hirschman, *The Strategy of Economic Development*, p. 122; for an empirical study, see Teitel and Thoumi.

The early development of manufactures in the northern United States, in contrast to delayed industrialization in the American South and in Latin America, with their much greater income inequalities, has been explained on these grounds.[12] The argument that an egalitarian distribution of income is favorable to growth is, of course, at odds with the more traditional view, which emphasizes the need for capital and therefore for savings, most readily accumulated by the rich.

When domestic income increases because of a boom in primary exports, a good part of it will be spent not on industrial goods but on food, especially in low-income countries. The concept of consumption linkage must therefore be extended to the additional domestic food production that is induced by the rise in exports. In Chile, for example, the rise in nitrate exports in the decades before World War I made for an expansion of wheat production in the Central Valley.[13] In Ecuador, mounting cocoa exports in the early decades of the century led similarly to an expansion of rice production to satisfy increases in domestic demand for food. Rice cultivation, once introduced, turned out to be well suited to some of the country's soils and climate, so that rice took over as an important foreign-exchange earner for Ecuador when the cocoa plantations were devastated by disease in the 1930s. It may therefore be not just luck if one primary product is rapidly followed by another as a mainstay of a country's exports: the consumption linkage dynamic will on occasion explain a good part of the story.

Recognition of the importance of consumption linkage has substantial implications for development policy. As long as only backward and forward linkages are taken into account, a development strategy that pays attention to the linkage concept is likely to have a proindustry bias. Traditional food-growing agriculture uses a low level of industrial inputs, such as machinery and fertilizer, and is therefore poor in backward linkage effects. Once agricultural techniques evolve, however, and particularly when

---

[12]See Baldwin.
[13]See Cariola and Sunkel.

consumption linkages are given their due, the expansion of agricultural incomes can be just as stimulating for overall growth as an industrial spurt. Precisely on this ground, recent reappraisals of development strategy favor a tilt of investment priorities toward agricultural improvement.[14] It is, of course, ironic that an analytical tool that originally served to justify the building up of industry in less developed areas should later be used for advocating a quite different development strategy. But this very shift testifies to the acceptance the linkage concept has gained: no matter what strategy is advocated, it is now felt necessary to make the case for it in terms of the vigorous linkage effects that would ensue.

FISCAL LINKAGE

Consumption linkage describes a familiar, spontaneous process: incomes are earned in a new activity and are then spent on goods that, while often imported at first, will eventually be produced domestically. One activity induces another through the market. But new activities can also be established by the state as it interferes with such market forces. The state can tap the flow of income accruing to the exporters through various forms of export taxes, or it can impose tariffs on the imported articles on which a good part of the new export-related incomes will be spent. The resulting fiscal receipts can then be used, among other things, to finance public or publicly supported investment projects. These sequences spell out a new class of *fiscal linkages*.[15] They are again rather roundabout and perhaps unreliable mechanisms compared to backward and forward linkages. Within that category, however, extraction (and subsequent expenditure) of revenue through export taxes has a relatively straightforward character and may be called *direct* fiscal linkage. The raising (and disposal) of fiscal receipts through tariffs on imports, on the

---

[14]See Adelman, and Mellor and Johnston.
[15]First so labeled by Pearson.

other hand, involves still more steps and is here labeled *indirect fiscal linkage*.

The choice by the state between direct and indirect fiscal linkage has largely depended on the kind of commodity that is being exported. Export taxes (direct fiscal linkage) have been prevalent in the case of primary commodities produced in enclave conditions—that is, in geographically isolated, often originally foreign-owned plantations, mines, and petroleum fields. It was the very concentration of production in an outlying area, its ownership by one or a few foreign firms, and the ease with which fiscal control over production and export volume could be established that invited the use of taxation at the source. When, on the contrary, the export commodity was produced over a wide, centrally located area by numerous domestic, politically influential producers—as in the case of coffee, cocoa, or other tropical crops—direct taxation was administratively difficult and politically inadvisable. Here the state resorted preferentially to indirect extraction of revenue by imposing tariffs on the imports that would flow into the country as a result of its primary exports.

The idea that the state should take advantage of some existing source of economic growth to stimulate growth elsewhere arose with particular strength in countries where the export product was a clearly *depletable* natural resource, such as guano or petroleum. It was supposed that the state had a special responsibility to use part of the wealth arising from the temporary "bonanza" for developing other "growth poles"[16] that could take over once the original source of export income had dried up. This is the meaning of the phrase "sow the petroleum" that was coined in Venezuela to justify various state-financed regional and industrial development schemes. Direct fiscal linkage has often had this aim of jumping, as it were, from an ongoing activity to a wholly different one, to be created ex nihilo, in contrast to the seemingly plodding backward and forward linkages where the new activities are in areas adjacent to the one already in existence. (By definition, an enclave activity is deprived of such adjacent opportun-

---

[16]See Perroux.

ities.) Unfortunately, such jumps into uncharted territory are very risky, so that direct fiscal linkage has sometimes resulted in white elephants.

But the state does not always act in this "creative" way: more frequently its economic activities have consisted in extending the infrastructure for ongoing economic activity, through investments in transportation (port facilities, railroads, and highways), communication, and, later, power generation as well as health and education. These types of public investment have often been characteristic of indirect fiscal linkage, with the state's revenue accruing primarily through tariffs on imports rather than through levies on exports. In these cases, the export articles that generate the dutiable imports are likely to be agricultural products whose cultivation could be further extended, and the state performs the comparatively low-risk task of facilitating it. At the same time, these public investments can have the result of accentuating the country's economic structure and of relegating it more firmly to its role as a supplier of certain primary products; in the course of colonial development, indirect fiscal linkage has in fact been an important mechanism acting in this manner.[17]

LINKAGE CONSTELLATIONS AND THE STAPLE THESIS

I have suggested here that different primary commodities may have affinities for different types or "bundles" of linkages, depending on their economic, geographic, social, and political conditions. For example, the enclave conditions under which certain commodities are produced favor direct fiscal linkage, but exclude by definition any substantial backward and forward linkages. (If such linkages appear, as when the production of crude petroleum is followed by the construction of oil refineries and petrochemical industries, then the resulting petroleum complex loses something of its enclave character.) Correlatively, the non-

---

[17]See Birnberg and Resnick.

enclave characteristics making for indirect rather than direct fiscal linkage—the export staple is produced by numerous domestic producers over wide areas and is marketed by a dense network of traders—should in due course also make for import-substituting industrialization (via the consumption linkages), and for backward linkages once agricultural technology becomes more advanced.

In this manner, the linkage approach has a great deal in common with the staple thesis developed by a group of Canadian economic historians. The most prominent member of the group, Harold Innis (1894–1952), showed in a series of meticulous and subtle studies how Canadian development—transportation facilities, settlement patterns, new economic activities—was shaped by the characteristics and requirements of specific primary commodities—from furs to codfish to timber, minerals, and wheat—that Canada was successively supplying to world markets. The virtue of the linkage approach in comparison to the staple thesis, with its detailed analysis of the impact of one commodity at a time, is that it supplies a few major categories that structure the inquiry and permit comparative analysis of the development paths which different staples are likely to trace out for the economies in which they are embedded. Naturally, a full accounting of the influence of any given staple in a specific environment will uncover a great many additional factors, some of which will be purely circumstantial, whereas others could point toward some further generalizable linkage varieties.

It is a basic tenet of the staple thesis that development of the periphery starts with the discovery of some staple that is in demand in the center. In contrast, the "development-of-underdevelopment" thesis has attempted to show that it was precisely the "successful" development of staples that was responsible for the impoverishment of the periphery: that the staple boom left nothing behind but a depressed area with depleted mines, exhausted soil, and impoverished subsistence agriculture.[18] The historical record contains a number of situations that seem to

---

[18]See Frank.

confirm this kind of analysis: the silver mines of Potosí in Bolivia, the "mining" of guano in Peru, and the sugar plantations of the Caribbean and of Brazil's Northeast. The linkage approach can resolve the apparent contradictions between the staple and the development-of-underdevelopment theses. Like the staple thesis, it was originally devised to explain different patterns of *growth,* but it is easily used to account for stagnation and immiserization. Some or all of the linkages may fail to materialize, and an inquiry into these failures once again permits a preliminary sorting out of some major conceivable reasons for such negative developments. In the case of staples produced in enclave conditions, for example, direct fiscal linkage may of course have appeared not at all or too feebly and too late. Alternatively, the linkage may have operated, but then could have led to misinvestments of the revenue: this was precisely the case in Peru, where revenues were extracted from the mid-nineteenth-century guano boom but were then spent on nonproductive railroad ventures.[19] In the case of agricultural staples, such as sugarcane, produced by slave labor on plantations, there may have been a failure of both indirect fiscal linkage and consumption linkage, since much of the income accrued to absentee owners and the income distributed to the work force was barely sufficient for subsistence and therefore provided little stimulus for additional food production on a commercial scale, for the importation of taxable consumer goods, and even less for their domestic production.

The various linkages, their possible failures, and their changing constellations make for an increasingly complex pattern of possibilities. Moreover, in some cases a linkage may be an obstacle to development, or at least to a certain kind of development, rather than an asset. This is the case when a bulky staple requires elaborate processing by technologically complex, capital-intensive methods to be transformed into a finished product. Such processing constitutes forward linkage, of course, but in the case of agricultural staples like sugarcane, it means that the growers themselves will often be unable to enter the processing phase,

---

[19]See Hunt.

which will therefore be occupied by outside entrepreneurs; in this manner growers of the staple will be locked into their agricultural activity. The opposite situation obtains when the staple needs little processing and is compact, with a comparatively high value per unit of weight. In this case the growers themselves—generally some member of the family—can handle the transportation and merchandising functions, acquiring new entrepreneurial and urban skills in the process. Actually what goes on here is that the absence of one kind of forward linkage—elaborate, capital-intensive processing—makes for the availability of another forward link, to the merchandising function, that can be taken advantage of directly by the producers. In the tropics, examples of this easy transition from agricultural production to activities in transportation, trade, and eventually to finance and industry are supplied by the story of coffee expansion in Colombia and Brazil. In parts of Greece and of some other Mediterranean countries, the production of olive oil, nuts and raisins, as McNeill has shown, has made for a similarly easy transition from rural to urban pursuits. The same holds true, with less happy overall results, for the production of marijuana, cocaine, and opium.

LINKAGES AND SOCIETY

The linkage constellations characteristic of a given staple not only spell out certain likely patterns of development (or stagnation) but also, through these patterns, influence the social order and political regime of countries where the staple is economically important. I have called the effort to trace such influences "micro-Marxism," the idea being that, in searching for the effects of the "productive forces" on the "relations of production," it may be fruitful to go considerably beyond the macromodes of production—feudal, capitalist, and so on—that Marx specified and stressed. This is particularly so for the countries of the periphery during the period of export-led growth when they were specialized in one or a very few primary product lines, with very different linkages and characteristics. But even in countries at a different stage of development, knowing the degree of compatibility or affinity between key economic activities and forms of social and political organization can be useful. For example, Wiles, a student of the centrally planned economies, has made a distinction between "left-wing crops" and "right-wing crops," pointing out that products requiring individual attention, such as grapes and certain fruits and vegetables, are particularly unsuitable for collectivized agriculture, in contrast to the more "left-wing" grains, where operations are standardized (with the important exception, one might add, of wet rice, whose cultivation definitely demands "tender loving care"). For the industrialized countries of the West it has been suggested that specific sectors (textiles, steel, chemicals, automobiles) which have been leaders at successive periods of industrial expansion, have each nurtured different "congenial" political forms or tendencies.[20]

Such micro-Marxist explorations can be insightful, but two qualifications are in order. First, there is no necessary one-to-one relationship between a specific economic activity and a "resulting" sociopolitical regime. The fact that there existed for a long time a mutually supportive and reinforcing relationship between sugarcane cultivation and slavery does not mean that sugarcane does not "fit" just as well into one or several very different social and political regimes. Nevertheless, the number of such fits may well be limited and some sociopolitical configurations could be definitely ill-suited to the development of a certain productive activity or technology.

Second, the causal connection between the productive activity, be it a staple or an industrial complex, and a sociopolitical regime does not flow in only one direction. The analysis has here primarily proceeded from the characteristics of a staple or an industry to their imprints on society and polity. But in many cases it is possible and inviting to reverse the direction of the inquiry: one might ask whether a certain kind of political regime is likely

---

[20]See Kurth.

to exhibit a strong preference for the promotion of a certain type of industrial development—such as a petrochemical complex.[21] Even in the famous case of the sugarcane-slavery complex, the connection probably works both ways: the prevailing technology of sugarcane lent itself to the introduction of an enslaved labor force, but the way of life the conquerors of the New World in the tropics wanted to establish for themselves made them look for the kind of economic activity that would best fulfill their wishes, and from among a number of possible land uses they chose the cultivation of cane by imported slaves as the most fulfilling.

The linkage concept, in short, invites the analyst to pay close attention to the differential technological and situational features of economic activities as a means of detecting how "one thing leads (or fails to lead) to another." But this focus does not prejudge either the nature or the principal direction of the causal links involved in the complex interactions among technology, ideology, institutions, and development. My contention is simply that the linkage approach has a number of interesting observations to make in this area. It thus challenges other approaches to propose alternative or supplementary interpretations.

Bibliographical References

Adelman, Irma. "Beyond Export-Led Growth." *World Development*, September 1984.

Baldwin, Robert E. "Patterns of Development in Newly Settled Regions." *Manchester School of Economics and Social Regions*, May 1956.

Birnberg, Thomas B., and Resnick, Stephen A. *Colonial Development: An Econometric Study*. New Haven, Conn.: Yale University Press, 1975.

Cariola, Carmen, and Sunkel, Oswaldo. "The Growth of the Nitrate Industry and Socioeconomic Change in Chile." In *The Latin American Economies: Growth and the Export Sector, 1880–1930*, edited by R. Cortés Conde and S. J. Hunt. New York: Holmes and Meier, 1985.

Corden, W. M. "The Structure of a Tariff System and the Effective Protection Rate." *Journal of Political Economy*, June 1966.

Dahmén, Erik. *Entrepreneurial Activity and the Development of Swedish Industry, 1919–1939*. 1950. Homewood, Ill.: Irwin, 1971.

Evans, Peter. "Generalized Linkages and Industrial Development." In *Development, Democracy and the Art of Trespassing: Essays in Honor of Albert O.*

---

[21]See Evans.

Hirschman, edited by A. Foxley et al. Notre Dame, Ind.: University of Notre Dame Press, 1986.

Frank, Andre Gunder. "The Development of Underdevelopment." *Monthly Review,* September 1966.

Furtado, Celso. "Industrialization and Inflation." *International Economic Papers,* 1967, no. 12.

García, Norberto E., and Marfán, Manuel. *Estructuras industriales y eslabonamientos de empleo.* Monografía sobre empleo 26. Santiago: PREALC-ILO, 1982.

Hirschman, Albert O. *The Strategy of Economic Development,* New Haven, Conn.: Yale University Press, 1958.

———. "The Political Economy of Import-Substituting Industrialization in Latin America." *Quarterly Journal of Economics,* February 1968; reprinted in *A Bias for Hope.* New Haven, Conn.: Yale University Press, 1971.

———. "A Generalized Linkage Approach to Development, with Special Reference to Staples." *Economic Development and Cultural Change,* supplement, 1977; "The Turn to Authoritarianism in Latin America and the Search for Its Economic Determinants." In *The New Authoritarianism in Latin America,* edited by D. Collier. Princeton, N.J.: Princeton University Press, 1979; reprinted in *Essays in Trespassing.* Cambridge: Cambridge University Press, 1981.

Hunt, Shane J. "Growth and Guano in Nineteenth-Century Peru." In *The Latin American Economies: Growth and the Export Sector, 1880–1930,* edited by R. Cortés Conde and S. J. Hunt. New York: Holmes and Meier, 1985.

Johnson, Harry G. *Economic Policies Toward Less Developed Countries.* Washington, D.C.: Brookings Institution, 1967.

Jones, Leroy P., ed. *Public Enterprise in Developing Countries.* Cambridge: Cambridge University Press, 1982.

Kafka, Alexandre. "The Theoretical Interpretation of Latin American Economic Development." In *Economic Development in Latin America,* edited by Howard S. Ellis. New York: St. Martin's Press, 1961.

Kaufman, Robert R. "Industrial Change and Authoritarian Rule in Latin America." In *The New Authoritarianism in Latin America,* edited by David Collier. Princeton, N.J.: Princeton University Press, 1979.

Kurth, James. "The Political Consequences of the Product Cycle: Industrial History and Political Outcomes." *International Organization,* Winter 1979.

Leff, Nathaniel H. "Industrial Organization and Entrepreneurship in the Developing Countries." *Economic Development and Cultural Change,* July 1978.

McNeill, William H. *The Metamorphosis of Greece Since World War II.* Oxford: Blackwell, 1978.

Mellor, John F., and Johnston, Bruce F. "The World Food Equation: Interrelations among Development, Employment and Food Consumption." *Journal of Economic Literature,* June 1984.

O'Donnell, Guillermo. "Reflexiones sobre las tendencias generales de cambio en el estado burocratico-autoritario." Buenos Aires, CEDES, 1975; also published in English in *Latin American Research Review,* Winter 1978.

Pearson, Scott R. *Petroleum and the Nigerian Economy.* Stanford, Calif.: Stanford University Press, 1970.

Perroux, François. *La coexistence pacifique*. Paris: Presses Universitaires de France, 1958.

Quarterly Journal of Economics, May 1976. Various articles on measurement of linkages.

Raj, K. N. "Linkages in Industrialization and Development Strategy: Some Basic Issues." *Journal of Development Planning*, no. 8 (1975).

Rostow, Walt W. *The Stages of Economic Growth*. Cambridge: Cambridge University Press, 1960.

Serra, José. "Three Mistaken Theses Regarding the Connection between Industrialization and Authoritarian Regimes." In *The New Authoritarianism in Latin America*, edited by David Collier. Princeton, N.J.: Princeton University Press, 1979.

Teitel, Simon, and Thoumi, Francisco. "From Import Substitution to Exports: The Recent Experience of Argentina and Brazil." *Economic Development and Cultural Change*, April 1986.

Watkins, Melville H. "A Staple Theory of Economic Growth." *Canadian Journal of Economics and Political Science*, May 1963.

Wiles, P. J. D. *Economic Institutions Compared*. New York: Wiley, 1977.

4. *Exit and Voice:*

AN EXPANDING SPHERE
OF INFLUENCE

A central place is held in economics and social science in general by principles and forces making for order or (to use a more ambitious term) equilibrium in economic and social systems. Disorder and disequilibrium are then understood as resulting from some malfunction of these principles or forces. The theory of the "social contract" in political science and the "law of supply and demand" in economics, with its ever more sophisticated versions, are explanations of order-disorder or equilibrium-disequilibrium of this sort. These explanations have typically been discipline-bound: they deal with either the political or the economic world. Since the two are interrelated, it would be useful to have a bridge between them. Such is the most ambitious claim of what I have called the exit-voice perspective. It makes clear that social actors who experience developing disorder have available to them two activist reactions and perhaps remedies: exit, or withdrawal from a relationship that one has built up as a buyer of merchandise or as a member of an organization such as a firm, a family, a political party, or a state; and voice, or the attempt at repairing and perhaps improving the relationship through an effort at communicating one's complaints, grievances, and proposals for improvement. The voice reaction belongs in good part to the political domain, since it has to do with the articulation and channeling of opinion, criticism, and protest. Much of the exit reaction involves the economic realm, as it is precisely the function of the markets for goods, services, and jobs to offer alternatives to consumers, buyers, and employees who are for various reasons dissatisfied with their current transaction partners.

I proposed and explored the exit-voice alternative in my book *Exit, Voice, and Loyalty* (1970). Much discussion followed, and attempts were made to apply the book's concepts to many areas of social life. Prompted in part by these reactions, I wrote additional papers on exit-voice in the 1970s (most were republished in my *Essays in Trespassing*. Here, I shall first recapitulate and, where necessary, reformulate the basic concepts of the original book, then briefly review the principal applications of the exit-voice polarity, as well as new problems that have surfaced.

BASIC CONCEPTS

Exit

By exit, I mean withdrawal from a relationship with a person or organization. If this relationship fulfills some vital function, then the withdrawal is possible only if the same relationship can be reestablished with another person or organization. Exit is therefore often predicated on the availability of choice, *competition*, and well-functioning *markets*.

Exit of customers serves as a signal to the management of firms and organizations that something is amiss. A search for causes and remedies may then be undertaken and a plan of action designed to restore performance adopted. This is one way in which markets and competition work to prevent decay, to maintain quality, and perhaps even to improve it.

Exit is a powerful but indirect and somewhat blunt way of alerting management to its failings. Most of the time, those customers and members of organizations who exit have no interest in improving them by their withdrawal, and exit does not provide management with much information on what is or has gone wrong.

Voice

The direct and more informative way of alerting management is to alert it: this is *voice*. It is, or should be, paramount in situations where exit either is not possible or is difficult, costly, and traumatic. This is so for certain primordial groupings one is born into—the family, the ethnic or religious community, the nation—or for those organizations one joins with the intention of staying for a prolonged period—school, marriage, political party, firm. With regard to buying and selling, voice should take over from exit when competition is weak or nonexistent, as in the case of goods and services being produced under monopolistic conditions, or when exit is expensive for both parties, as in certain interfirm relations.

Unlike exit in well-functioning markets, voice is never easy; it can even be dangerous. Many organizations and their agents are not at all keen on having their members tell them about their shortcomings, and the voicers often expose themselves to reprisals.[1] Even in the absence of reprisals, the cost of voice to an individual member in terms of time and effort will often exceed any conceivable benefit. Frequently, moreover, the success of channeling individual voices requires members to join together, so that voice formation depends on the potential for collective action.

In spite of these problems, voice exists or, rather, it has come into being. Its history is to a considerable extent the history of the right to dissent, of due process,[2] of safeguards against reprisal, and of the advance of trade unions and of consumer and many other organizations articulating the demands of individuals and groups. Similarly, the history of exit is the history of the broadening of the market, of the right to move freely, to emigrate, to be a conscientious objector, to divorce, and so on. Being two basic, complementary ingredients of democratic freedom, the right to exit and the right to voice have on the whole been enlarged or restricted jointly. Yet there are important instances of periods,

[1] See Birch.
[2] See Evan.

countries, and economic-political regimes that are marked by unilateral advances or retreats of either the one or the other. Interesting comparative accounts for Europe have been provided by Rokkan and Finer.

Interaction of Exit and Voice

In some circumstances exit is paramount as a reaction to discontent and in others voice is, but frequently both mechanisms are available jointly, in which case they may either reinforce or undercut each other. The availability and threat of exit on the part of an important customer or group of members may powerfully reinforce their voice. On the other hand, the actual recourse to exit will often diminish the volume of voice that would otherwise be forthcoming and, should the organization be more sensitive to voice than to exit, the stage could be set for cumulative deterioration. For example, after an incipient deterioration of public schools or inner cities, the availability of private schools or suburban housing would lead, via exit, to further deterioration—a turn of events that might have been prevented if the parents sending their children to private school or the inner-city residents moving to the suburbs had instead used their voice to press for reform. In their aggregate effect, individual exit decisions are harmful—an instance of the "tyranny of small decisions"—also because they are usually made only on the basis of a short-run private-interest calculus, and do not take into account the "public bad" that will be inflicted, even on those who exit, by decaying inner cities and segregated education.[3]

These kinds of situations are sufficiently numerous and important to be of interest not only as curious paradoxes showing that under some circumstances the availability of exit (i.e., of competition) could have undesirable effects. In this connection, I stressed the value of loyalty as a factor that might delay overrapid exit. Loyalty would make a member reluctant to leave an organization upon the slightest manifestation of decline even though rival organizations were available. Provided it is not "blind," loy-

---

[3]See Levin, and Breneman.

alty would also activate voice as loyal members are strongly motivated to save "their" organization once deterioration has passed some threshold.

This argument could be formulated in terms of the concept of trust. Absence of trust would make for excessive instability through massive desertions from organizations whose performance is declining. The presence of trust would counteract such instability; provided, once again, that it is not unlimited or "blind," it will help to enlist the voice of the organization's members in the tasks of recovery and reform.[4]

Just as there are some organizations where deterioration will primarily provide exit when voice would be more conducive to recovery, so is it conceivable that in other organizations deterioration gives rise routinely to voice, even though exit might put on more pressure to reform (or pass from the scene). This tends to be the case for governments—ministers and high officials, even though disaffected, often find it difficult to resign and will often invent all kinds of arguments why they have to stay on just a little while longer, while assuaging their conscience by speaking up within the councils of government.

The difficulties of combining exit and voice in an optimal manner are in a sense "problems of the rich": they relate to situations and societies where exit and voice are both forthcoming more or less abundantly, but where, for best results, one would wish for a different mix. Historically more frequent are cases where exit and voice are both in short supply, in spite of many reasons for discontent and unhappiness. There is no doubt, as many commentators have pointed out,[5] that passivity, acquiescence, inaction, withdrawal, and resignation have held sway much of the time over wide areas of the social world. This is largely the result of repression of both exit and voice—a repression that has flourished though all human organizations could put the feedback from them both to good use.

The persistence of inaction and the passages from passivity

---

[4]See Barber.

[5] See Bruinsma; Kolarska and Aldrich; and Laponce.

to activism and back again are of course important areas of inquiry for the social sciences. But just because of the importance of this topic it is justified to focus separately on the different *forms* (such as exit and voice) that activism can take and on their interplay.

Problems in Voice Formation

The development of voice among customers of firms or members of organizations poses a number of problems that I had not fully explored. Critics such as Barry have asserted that, in my endeavor to present voice as a ready alternative to exit, I understated the difficulties of voice formation. In examining this issue it is useful to start with the extreme no-voice case: the authoritarian state which is dedicated to repressing and suppressing voice. This situation has suggested to O'Donnell the useful distinction between *horizontal* and *vertical* voice: the latter is an actual communication, complaint, petition, or protest addressed to the authorities by a citizen or, more frequently, an organization representing a group of citizens; the former is the utterance and exchange of opinion, concern, and criticism *among* citizens— once known as the "murmuring of the people," it is today regularly ascertained (in more open societies) through opinion polls revealing, for example, the approval rating of presidents, prime ministers or mayors. Horizontal voice is a necessary precondition for the mobilization of vertical voice. It is the earmark of the more frightful authoritarian regimes that they suppress not only vertical voice—any ordinary tyranny does that—but horizontal voice as well. The suppression of horizontal voice is generally the side-effect of the terrorist methods used openly by such regimes in dealing with its real and imagined enemies. For once, this side effect is intended: it is greatly welcomed by regimes who hope to gain in power and stability by thus converting citizens into isolated, wholly private, and narrowly self-centered individuals.

O'Donnell's work on horizontal voice has a bearing on the prospects for voice in general. For vertical voice to come about— that is, for members of an organization to engage management in meaningful dialogue and bargaining—it is frequently necessary for members to forge a tie among themselves and to create an organization that will agitate for their demands. But the hoped-for result of this collective and vertical voice is a freely available public good; hence, so goes the critical argument, self-interested, "rational" individuals may well withhold their contribution to the voice enterprise in the expectation that others will take on the entire burden. Important as it is, this "free-ride" argument has its limitations. First of all, it is addressed only to vertical voice, which it mistakenly equates (as I did in my book) with voice in general. Horizontal voice is not subject to the strictures of the free-ride argument: it is free, spontaneous activity of men and women in society, akin to breathing, and extraordinary violence must be deployed to suppress it. Under ordinary circumstances, horizontal voice is continuously generated and has an effect even without becoming vertical. This is obviously the case for approval ratings of important public figures, but in general, managers of organizations cannot help noticing and reacting to members' critical opinions and hostile moods, whether or not organized protest movements break out. That the planned economies of Eastern Europe function to the extent they do has been explained on precisely this ground, as in the following statement:

> One thing is clear if one considers the system by itself: it just cannot function. But if one looks at reality, there is evidence that it does function—poorly, to be sure, but the machine somehow works, if creakily and laboriously. That which in theory cannot work, does work in practice—how is it possible? Life gave the answer. When workers are handed defective tools in the morning they are angry all day long, their income suffers, and they will gripe about it in the evening [upon returning the tools]. Eventually the man in charge of handing out the tools is fed up with being a butt of insults and will see to it that the tools are in acceptable shape.[6]

Another limitation of the free-ride argument lies in its axiomatic assumption that individuals will always adopt a purely in-

---

[6]See Bender, p. 30; my translation.

strumental attitude in their activities. Just because the desired result of collective voice is typically a *public* good—or, better, some aspect of the *public* happiness—participation in voice provides an alternative to purely self-centered, instrumental action. It therefore has the powerful attractions of those activities that are marked by the fusion of striving and attaining, and can also be understood as an investment in individual or group identity.[7] Such considerations make it likely that voice is subject to greater instability than exit: participation in, and withdrawal from, collective action might come in waves, with large numbers of persons shifting from instrumental to noninstrumental behavior and back again.

Voicing behavior is subject to other complexities, as Bourdieu has shown. Suppose members of an organization A have some grievances and choose to voice them rather than to leave. Channeling their voice so as to be able to deal with A's managers will often require establishing a separate organization, B. But B's performance may give rise to renewed unhappiness among its members, who will confront the exit-voice dilemma all over again, this time in relation to B. Bourdieu's formulation is somewhat reminiscent of Roberto Michels's "Iron Law of Oligarchy" (1915), according to which all organizations—Michels was particularly concerned with political parties and trade unions—are bound to come under the domination of small cliques of bureaucrats and to be run in their interest. Bourdieu, if I understand him correctly, is not so pessimitic: for him the encroachment of the oligarchy and the consequent diversion of the organization from its original purposes are *avoidable* dangers, provided members are watchful and ready to react through new exit or voice moves.

It must be granted that the voice option is typically subject to this sort of, one hopes not infinite, regress. Much of the attraction of exit comes from the fact that it makes a clean, once-and-for-all break: voice, particularly vertical voice, is a laborious and never-ending affair—like the struggle for liberty and justice.

---

[7]See chapter 6, and Pizzorno.

SOME AREAS OF APPLICATION

Trade Unions

In economics, the major application of the exit-voice theme, unforeseen by me when I first advanced it, has been the exhaustive analysis of trade unions as collective voice by Freeman and Medoff in their book *What Do Unions Do?* Instead of looking at unions as a monopolistic device raising wages for unionized workers beyond the "market-clearing" equilibrium level or—what amounts to much the same zero-sum interpretation in different language—as a tool in the class struggle serving to reduce the degree of exploitation, the book finds that a major function of unions is that of channeling information to management about workers' aspirations and complaints. Collective voice, in the form of union bargaining, is far more efficient in conveying information about workers' discontent—and in doing something about it—than individual decisions to quit, for the simple reason that voice carries more information than exit. In line with my major initial hypothesis, the presence of union voice is shown to reduce exit—that is, costly labor turnover. For this reason alone, it increases labor productivity. Moreover, the fringe benefits, workplace practices, seniority rules, and so on that unions negotiate often improve working conditions to such an extent that their cost to management is more than offset by increased labor productivity. There are of course situations where unions play zero-sum games: in particular, they are able to capture for their members a portion of the monopoly profits of highly concentrated industries. But Freeman and Medoff find that these situations are less important than those where the voice function of unions brings benefits to workers, to the economy as a whole, and occasionally even to management.

Markets and Hierarchies

Renewed attention has been given in recent years to the question why some kinds of economic activity are carried on by independent firms that are interrelated through the market while others are organized along bureaucratic and hierarchical lines.

The question can be asked, for example, with regard to suppliers of parts or materials: under what conditions will they be and remain independent, and when will they become a subdivision of a vertically integrated firm? In accounting for hierarchy, Williamson's influential approach has directed attention to such matters as uncertainty about the evolution of the market and the technology, and in particular to asymmetric availability of information to buyer and seller, creating opportunities for deceitful behavior. In other words, hierarchy is considered to be superior to markets whenever there is a need for a sustained and frank dialogue between the contracting parties. Critics of this position such as Granovetter and Eccles have made two interrelated points: (1) relations between independent firms, such as contractors and subcontractors, are often quite effective in discouraging malfeasance; and (2) hierarchy frequently leads to characteristic patterns of concealment and control evasion. Moreover, industry structure varies substantially from one country to another as well as within the same country over time: in Japan, for example, as Sabel has shown, subcontracting is much more widely practiced than in the West, and in Italy subcontracting has spread in the last ten or twenty years.

A formulation in terms of exit-voice is helpful here. The characteristics that are alleged to justify hierarchy are incomplete information, considerable apprenticing of one firm by the other, and openings for "opportunistic" (i.e., dishonest) behavior. All make for situations in which the firms contracting together must intensively consult with, and watch over, each other. *But this need for voice does not necessarily imply that hierarchy is in order.* Whether voicing is done best within the same organization or from one independent firm to another is by no means a foregone conclusion.[8] Moreover, when the two parties are independent and resort a great deal to voice, the possibility of exit often looms, and the implicit threat of exit may carry as much clout as that of sanctions in a hierarchy.

The argument for hierarchy in cases where resort to voice

---

[8]See Granovetter.

must be frequent probably arises from thinking of market relationships only in terms of an ideal, highly competitive, anonymous market, where exit is all-powerful and voice wholly absent. But most real markets involve voice: commerce *is* communication, and is premised on frequent and close contact of the contracting parties who deliver promises, trust them, and engage in mutual adjustment of claims and complaints—all of this was implicit in the eighteenth-century notion of *doux commerce*. Adam Smith even conjectured that it was man's ability to communicate through speech that lies at the source of his "propensity to truck and barter." How odd, then, to adduce the need for frequent and intensive communication as an argument for hierarchy.

Public Services

The organization of public services represents a privileged area for the application of exit-voice reasoning—significantly the exit-voice idea had its origin in my analysis of a public service in trouble, the Nigerian railroads. Public services are typically sold or delivered by a single public or publicly regulated supplier, for various reasons: (1) some services (railroads, postal services, electric power, etc.) are supplied by a technical or legal monopoly; and (2) some services (education, health) are not paid for directly, because all citizens regardless of income are considered to be entitled to them—hence they cannot be supplied through the market; (3) in some cases society holds that a service should be supplied in conditions of uniform, publicly controlled quality regardless of the variation of consumer preferences. For example, one argument for public education, particularly in a democracy with diverse ethnic and religious groups, has been that it is desirable for all children to pass through a "common educational experience," that is, for all schools to instill basic civic values and to offer uniform instruction in certain elementary fields.[9]

Since the production of most public services is thus deprived of the "discipline of the market," problems in maintaining productive efficiency and quality arise necessarily. One obvious way

[9]See Levin.

of mitigating these problems is to reintroduce market pressures in some fashion. For example, when certain categories of goods and services are to be made available either to all citizens regardless of their income or to some deprived social groups, the state and its agencies may refrain from producing or distributing these goods directly, and instead issue special purpose money or *vouchers* enabling the beneficiaries to acquire the goods or services through ordinary market channels; the voucher system reintroduces the market and the possibility of exit into a situation from which they seemed to have been excluded. A particularly successful example of the voucher system is the distribution of food stamps to poor persons in the United States. Instead of creating and administering its own food-distribution network, the state hands out vouchers (food stamps) which the beneficiaries can then use at existing, competitive commercial outlets they already know about.

In part because of the success of this program and in part because of the belief in "market solutions" as a sovereign remedy for all that ails government programs, voucher schemes have been proposed for many other public services, from education to low-cost housing to certain health services. But their appropriateness largely turns on the characteristics of the good or service that is to be provided. According to one survey the voucher (or exit) solution works best under the following conditions: (1) when there are widespread differences in taste that are recognized as legitimate; (2) when people are well informed about the quality of the goods and services they want and can easily compare and evaluate them; (3) when purchases are relatively small in relation to income and recurrent, so that buyers can learn from experience and easily switch from one brand and supplier to another; and (4) when there are many competing suppliers.

These conditions are present in the case of foodstuffs, but much less so in the case of, say, health and educational services. Here the buyers of the services are often ill-informed about quality, there are few suppliers, and comparison shopping is complicated and even impossible in the case of some very important decisions. Hence, voucher systems are likely to run into difficulties; they may even be inappropriate when, as already noted for the case of basic education, a certain uniformity of the product is considered desirable from society's point of view, regardless of individual preferences. Then, the development of voice constitutes an important alternative strategy for assuring and maintaining product quality. In other words, the beneficiaries of the public services—in some cases, their parents, or relatives or friends—should be induced to become active, individually or collectively, on their own behalf or on behalf of their wards. As always, development of voice is arduous if the people are apathetic or passive, and also if it is—shortsightedly, but none the less actively—resisted and perhaps repressed by the organizations that have been set up to deliver the services. Nevertheless, many proposals and attempts have been made to introduce more voice into the administration of both health and educational services.[10]

I had originally insisted on the seesaw character of exit and voice interventions in these fields. Education and health systems especially seemed exposed to the danger that premature exit—of the potentially most influential members—would undermine voice. The opposite relation may also occur, however, for the opening up of the exit perspective may serve to strengthen voice: parents who have been passive because they were feeling powerless and fearing reprisal may feel empowered for the first time once they are given vouchers that can be used "against" the schools currently attended by their children, and they will be readier than before to speak out with regard to desirable changes.

Spatial Mobility (Migration) and Political Action

Another substantial area of exit-voice applications opens up when exit is taken in the literal, spatial sense, that is, in the sense of physically moving away from a troublesome situation. Here exit-voice boils down to the familiar flight-or-fight alternative. While often institutionalized among nomadic groups, this alternative is not always available in sedentary societies, where the

---

[10]See Stevens, and Klein.

normal and traditional choice is to fight or submit in silence, as Hamlet knew well (" . . . to suffer the slings and arrows of outrageous fortune, or to take arms against a sea of troubles . . . "). The option of removing oneself from an oppressive environment has become available on a massive scale only in modern times, with the extraordinary advances in transportation and the *uneven* opening up of economic opportunity, religious tolerance, and political freedom. Where the option has existed, one can see the interaction of exit and voice in three principal types of migration: (1) from the countryside to the city, the oldest and no doubt largest of modern migrations, which has almost exhausted itself in the advanced industrial countries, but still proceeds massively and at high speed in much of the Third World; (2) from the city to the suburbs, which was most intense in the United States during the 1950s and 1960s, owing to the spread of the automobile and also to the large-scale migration of blacks and Hispanics *into* the cities, which led to the out-migration of whites; (3) finally, of course, international migration, with its numerous economic and political determinants and constraints. (Under this last rubric, the international movement of capital also deserves attention.) Looking at exit-voice interplay in these diverse settings, it is possible, on the basis of the numerous studies now available, to distinguish three distinct patterns:

1. In accordance with my basic hypothesis, exit-migration deprives the geographical unit that is left behind (countryside, city, nation) of many of its more activist residents, including potential leaders, reformers, or revolutionaries. Exit weakens voice and thus reduces the prospects for advance, reform, or revolution in the unit that is being left; it may also cause a process of cumulative decline to take hold there.

Something of this pattern can be observed in all three types of migration. Massive rural-urban migration reduces the potential as well as the need for land reforms, which the voice of the countryside might otherwise have precipitated.[11] The recent city-

---

[11]See Huntington and Nelson, pp. 103 ff.

to-suburbs migration in the United States has led, at least initially, to cumulative deterioration in the affected urban areas in spite of, and in some cases because of, reduced density. And the large emigration from Europe to the United States in the nineteenth century and up to World War I probably functioned as a political safety-valve for the rapidly industrializing European societies of that period, as has been shown for Italy.[12] In a similar vein, Frederick Jackson Turner invoked the possibility of westward migration within the United States to explain the lack of a militant working-class movement in that country. At times, the voice-weakening effect of exit is consciously utilized by the authorities: permitting, favoring, or even ordering the exit of enemies or dissidents has long been one—comparatively civilized—means for autocratic rulers to rid themselves of their critics, a practice revived on a large scale by Castro's Cuba and, on a more selective basis, by the Soviet Union in the post-Stalin era.

2. But the basic seesaw pattern—the more exit, the less voice—does not exhaust the rich historical material. I noted before that (maddeningly for the neatness of the scheme) the availability of exit can in fact reinforce voice because it confers new power and assurance on voice. The mechanism through which it is strengthened rather than weakened as a result of exit is distinctive in the case of migration. In some societies the accumulated social pressures could be so strong that authoritarian political controls will be relaxed more readily only if a certain amount of migration takes place concurrently. This is what happened in the fifty years prior to World War I when the franchise and other civil rights were extended in many European states from which large contingents of people were departing. In other words, the state accommodated some of the pressures toward democratization because it could be reasonably surmised, in part as a result of emigration, that opening the door slightly to voice would not blow away the whole structure. A similar positive relation between exit and voice may exist today in such southern European countries as Spain,

---

[12]See MacDonald.

Portugal, and Greece: here the large-scale emigration of workers to northern Europe may also have eased the transition to a more democratic (more vociferous) order.

A related reasoning applies to rural-urban migration: rather than making land reform obsolete, it may change land reform from being impossibly disruptive to being politically feasible— from the point of view of the political power holders. After a long period of large-scale emigration from the countryside and concurrent agrarian transformations, perhaps only a few hard-core areas with inequitable and uneconomic land tenure arrangements are left, and it then becomes possible and perhaps inviting to tackle these fairly well circumscribed problems and even to compensate the owners—something that is impossible with a reform that covers the major portion of a country's agricultural land. In other words, here also voice may be listened to when, because of prior or concurrent exits, it is no longer likely to have cataclysmic consequences.

3. Over and above these direct consequences of various types of migration, exit-voice theory invites us to look for remedial or preventive responses to large-scale emigration made by the entity that is being left. A firm losing customers or a political party losing members will normally search for the reasons for its decline in fortune and then determine a strategy for recovery. Some such reaction might be expected in the case of physical emigration, but actually it is not easy to identify. In the case of rural-urban migration, for example, there is usually no organized entity called the "countryside" that would register the flight from it and undertake corrective action. With migration from city to suburb, the situation is similar: although here an administrative entity exists, there is usually not very much that it can accomplish to make staying in the city more attractive and to retain its more affluent taxpayers. Projects to improve public services and police protection have of course frequently been proclaimed. Moreover, cities have often lobbied with the state government to obtain funds for such purposes as the "revitalization of deteriorating neighborhoods," and these programs have had some success. On the whole, however, the individual decisions of millions of peo-

ple to move to the suburbs have not been substantially modified by such official, usually rather timid, attempts to stem the tide.[13]

The analogy to the firm is—or should be—most applicable when the geographic entity losing residents is the state, which is after all a highly organized, self-reflective body with considerable means of action. I have already noted the possibility that emigration relieves a country's economic or political stress, is therefore *welcome,* and may even be encouraged by the state. But massive emigration is at some point bound to be viewed as dangerous: it will no longer be compared to a "safety valve," but rather to a dangerous "loss of blood." Just like a business firm, the state may then take measures to make itself more attractive to its citizens. One example of this reaction is the national plan for economic recovery and industrialization adopted by Ireland in 1958, in the midst of very high levels of emigration, mostly to England.[14] Similarly, the pioneering welfare-state measures of the late nineteenth and early twentieth century, starting in Bismarck's Germany in the 1880s and then spreading to the Scandinavian countries and Great Britain, were all taken in countries with high rates of overseas emigration. These measures can therefore be interpreted as attempts of states to make themselves more attractive to their exit-prone citizens.[15]

Faced with mass exit, the state has one option that is not available to other organizations and to firms: by virtue of its territorial authority and by using its monopoly of force, it can lock up its members within its own borders. While not particularly constructive, this can be an efficient way of curbing exit, as has been demonstrated by the German Democratic Republic and the other countries in the Soviet orbit, including of course the Soviet Union itself.

A word must be added on capital movement and capital flight. The increasing importance of movable capital was first com-

---

[13]See Fainstein and Fainstein.
[14]See Burnett.
[15]See Kuhnle.

mented upon in the eighteenth century. Montesquieu and Adam Smith both thought that the threat of exit on the part of this capital could usefully prevent the state from taking arbitrary and confiscatory measures against the legitimate interests of commerce and industry. The threat of exit or exit itself was expected to function, like the customer's exit from a firm, as a curb on state misconduct. While this relationship is still pertinent, exit of capital is often less constructive today. In the more peripheral capitalist countries the owners of capital have become fully alive to the possibility of removing part of their holdings to the United States or other reliable places in case they become unhappy about what they call the local "investment climate." In this manner, capital exit (or flight) will often be practiced on a large scale as soon as the state undertakes some, perhaps long overdue, reforms with respect to such matters as land tenure or fiscal equity. Instead of preventing arbitrary and ill-considered policies, exit can thus complicate and render more hazardous certain *needed* reforms. Moreover, exit undercuts voice: as long as the capitalists are able to remove their patrimony, they will have that much less incentive to raise their voice for the purpose of making a responsible contribution to national problem-solving. As I have argued elsewhere, capital mobility and propensity to exit may thus be a major reason why states in the capitalist periphery are feeble and unstable.

Political Parties

I put forward two principal propositions with regard to the dynamics of political parties in a democracy:

1. In a two-party system, the tendency of both parties to move toward the nonideological center in order to capture the (allegedly) voluminous middle-of-the-road vote is countered by party members and militants who are on the ideological fringes, who have "nowhere else to go," but who just because of that are maximally motivated to exert influence inside the party by forceful uses of voice—including, for example, threats of passivity during election campaigns;

2. In a multiparty system, with the ideological distance from one party to the next presumed shorter than in a two-party system, dissatisfaction with party performance is more likely to lead to exit. In two-party systems, voice plays the more important role, since switching to the other party requires too big an ideological jump. One may infer that parties in a two-party system will exhibit more internal divisions, but also more internal democracy and less bureaucratic centralism, than parties in a multiple-party system.

The first of these propositions has been strongly supported by events subsequent to the publication of my book. At that time, only the nomination of Barry Goldwater to be the standard-bearer of the Republican party in 1964 could be cited in support. Since then, additional evidence has accumulated: from the nomination by the Democrats of George McGovern to contend the presidential election in 1972 to the increasing power of the more radical wing of the Labour Party in Great Britain and the ascendancy of Margaret Thatcher within the Conservative party and, in the United States, of Ronald Reagan among the Republicans. While several factors have played a role in these events, of course, the thesis that in a two-party system the two parties would increasingly converge toward some middle ground has been amply disconfirmed.

The second proposition on political parties that I put forward has not fared so well. The conclusion that dissatisfaction with party performance will lead to voice in parties of two-party systems and to exit in those operating in multiple-party systems was based on an extremely simple model, with just one spectrum of opinion—left to right—where ideological distance between adjoining parties was presumed to be the shorter the more parties there were. Actually, of course, many other dimensions for political alignment exist, especially in democracies with old cleavages along ethnic, linguistic, and religious lines, so that the distances among the several parties may actually be longer than that between the parties of two-party systems. Under these conditions, the exit-voice logic will in fact predict that member participation (voice) in parties of multiparty systems will also be vigorous and exit infrequent.[16]

In a recent work, Kernell stresses another complicating factor. In two-party systems, exit is a particularly powerful move for dissatisfied members, as by casting their vote for the other party they are doubling its impact; in multiparty systems they cannot be sure of doing so, except when a dominant opposition party exists (which means that in effect a two-party system prevails). Hence, in case of disappointment with the performance of one's own party in a two-party system, there could arise a special temptation to switch to the other party so as to punish one's own, rather than to work for change from within. Such a strategically motivated preference for exit is likely to come to the fore primarily when a party in power is perceived as having seriously mishandled its mandate. Under the circumstances, the prospect of being able to punish the party retrospectively might overcome party loyalty and past ideological commitment. This constellation was an important factor in the sharp defeat of the Democratic ticket in the 1980 presidential elections in the United States.

Marriage and Divorce

Modern marriage is one of the simplest illustrations of the exit-voice alternative. When a marriage is in difficulty, either the partners can make an attempt, usually through a great deal of voicing, to reconstruct their relationship, or they can divorce. The complexities of the interplay between exit and voice are well in evidence here. Just as the threat of strike in labor-management relations, so is the threat of divorce important in inducing the parties to "bargain seriously." But as exit becomes ever easier, less costly, and perhaps even profitable to one of the parties[17] it will undermine voice: rather than being an action of last resort (like strikes, which are always costly), divorce can become the automatic response to marital difficulty with less and less effort made at communication and reconciliation.

---

[16]See my *Essays in Trespassing,* and Lorwin.

[17]See Weitzman for this point and the following statements on divorce in the United States.

This is exactly what appears to have happened in the United States during the last fifteen years, that is, since I first stated that "the expenditure of time, money and nerves" necessitated by complicated divorce procedures serves the useful, if unintended, purpose of "stimulating voice in deteriorating, yet recuperable organizations which would be prematurely destroyed through free exit." In 1970 California adopted a new no-fault law on divorce which spread, though often in attenuated form, to most other states. The California law drastically altered divorce procedures: instead of requiring proof that one of the parties was guilty of some specific type of behavior constituting grounds for divorce, the new law permitted divorce when both *or just one* of the two parties asserted that the marriage had irretrievably broken down. While the number of divorces had long been rising, their increase accelerated after 1970 to the point where today one of every two new marriages is likely to end in divorce.

From the point of view of voice, the most striking aspect of the new legal situation is the abolition of the need to obtain a spouse's agreement to divorce. The possibility of a unilateral decision, of just "walking out," is symbolic of the way in which the California law undercuts the recourse to voice. Other states have not gone quite so far: divorcing couples must often decide jointly whether to go the no-fault route or whether to invoke the traditional fault-based procedure. In yet other states, an immediate divorce can be had only via the traditional fault-based system, whereas the no-fault divorce, which dispenses the parties from agreeing on anything, even on the "breakdown" itself, requires them to establish separate residences and to wait for the expiration of a statutory period of time.

The pendulum has thus swung quite far in the direction of facilitating exit and thereby weakening voice. This was, of course, a reaction against the many abuses of the older fault-based system, which required costly and degrading adversarial proceedings and in effect discriminated against the poor: only middle- and upper-middle-class people could afford divorce. But the framers of the new legislation probably did not realize the extent to which the earlier obstacles to divorce indirectly encouraged attempts at mending the so easily frayed conjugal relationship and how much the new freedom to exit would torpedo such attempts.

The new statutes appear to mirror the popular misconception that the married state is either total bliss or unmitigated bust and hell. Actually, of course, the institution of marriage must be endowed with some degree of solidity precisely because most of the time it is neither, but is replete with recurrent conflict that needs to be managed and brought, as I have written, "routinely into the open without risking, each time, the survival of the relationship." In disregard of this reality, the California no-fault law is the equivalent of issuing to each newly married person a voucher that permits one partner to "turn in" the other without substantial cost and without having to justify himself (herself). The voucher solution is even more inappropriate for securing the optimal supply of sexual and companionship services than was earlier shown to be the case for health and educational services.

Adolescent Development

Here is another family situation for whose analysis a formulation in terms of exit and voice has been found useful. As Carol Gilligan shows, adolescent development has often been portrayed as a process through which the "dependent" child becomes an "independent" adult through progressive "detachment" from the parents. Freud saw this as "one of the most significant, but also one of the most painful psychical accomplishments of the pubertal period . . . a process that alone makes possible the opposition, which is so important for the progress of civilization, between the new generation and the old." Here is a celebration of exit: Freud's statement neglects a complementary aspect and task of adolescent development, which is to maintain and enrich the bond with the older generation through continued, if conflict-ridden, communication. In other words, voice is also important in transforming the adolescent's relationship to the parents. The peculiar poignancy of the adolescent-parent conflict resides, in fact, in the impossibility of relying wholly on voice to resolve it: given the closeness of the relationship, a full accord that would be the outcome of successful voicing risks ending up in incest, since the "meeting of minds would suggest a meeting of bodies," as Gilligan writes. It is because of the incest taboo that exit must be part of the solution, but different generations of adolescents are likely to achieve emancipation by practicing very different mixes of exit and voice. Moreover, Gilligan stresses that the balance of exit and voice differs according to gender: girls, who place a greater value than boys on continued attachment to the family and are therefore less attracted to the masculine ideal of independence-isolation, experience a greater tension between exit and voice.

With this imaginative use of the exit-voice concept, the outer limits of its sphere of influence may have been reached.

Bibliographical References

Barber, Bernardo. *The Logic and Limits of Trust.* New Brunswick, N.J.: Rutgers University Press, 1983.

Barry, Brian. "Review article: 'Exit, Voice, and Loyalty.'" *British Journal of Political Science,* February 1974.

Bender, Peter. *Das Ende des ideologischen Zeitalters.* Berlin: Severin und Siedler, 1981.

Birch, A. H. "Economic Models in Political Science: The Issue of 'Exit, Voice, and Loyalty.'" *British Journal of Political Science,* January 1975.

Bourdieu, Pierre. "The Antinomies of Collective Voice." In *Development, Democracy, and the Art of Trespassing: Essays in Honor of Albert O. Hirschman,* edited by A. Foxley et al. Notre Dame, Ind.: University of Notre Dame Press, 1986.

Breneman, David W. "Where Would Tuition Tax Credit Take Us? Should we Agree to Go?" In *Public Dollars for Private Schools,* edited by T. James and H. M. Levin. Philadelphia: Temple University Press, 1983.

Bridge, Gary. "Citizen Choice in Public Services: Voucher Systems." In *Alternatives for Delivering Public Services,* edited by E. S. Savas. Boulder, Colo.: Westview, 1977.

Bruinsma, Freek. "The (Non-) Assertion of Welfare Rights: Hirschman's Theory Applied." *Acta Politica,* 1980, no. 3.

Burnett, Nicholas R. "Emigration and Modern Ireland." Ph.D. diss., School of Advanced International Studies, Johns Hopkins University, 1976.

Coleman, James S. "Introducing Social Structure into Economic Analysis." *American Economic Review,* May 1984.

Eccles, Robert G. "The Quasifirm in the Construction Industry." *Journal of Economic Behavior and Organization,* December 1981.

Evan, William M. "Power, Conflict, and Constitutionalism in Organizations." *Social Science Information,* 1975, no. 1.

Fainstein, Norman I. and Susan S. "Mobility, Community, and Participation: The

American Way Out." In *Residential Mobility and Public Policy*, edited by E. G. Moore and W. A. V. Clark. Beverly Hills, Calif.: Sage, 1980.

Finer, Samuel E. "State-Building, State Boundaries and Border Control in the Light of the Rokkan-Hirschman Model." *Social Science Information*, 1974, nos. 4–5.

Freeman, Richard B., and Medoff, James L. *What Do Unions Do?* New York: Basic Books, 1984.

Freud, Sigmund. "Three Essays on the Theory of Sexuality." 1905. In *Complete Psychological Works*. Vol. 7. London: Hogarth, 1953. Cited in Gilligan.

Gilligan, Carol. "Exit-Voice Dilemmas in Adolescent Development." In *Development, Democracy, and the Art of Trespassing: Essays in Honor of Albert O. Hirschman*, edited by A. Foxley et al. Notre Dame, Ind.: University of Notre Dame Press, 1986.

Granovetter, Mark. "Economic Action and Social Structure: A Theory of Embeddedness." *American Journal of Sociology*, November 1985.

Hirschman, Albert O. *Exit, Voice, and Loyalty: Responses to Decline in Firms, Organizations, and States*. Cambridge, Mass.: Harvard University Press, 1970.

―――. *The Passions and the Interests: Political Arguments for Capitalism Before Its Triumph*. Princeton, N.J.: Princeton University Press, 1977.

―――. *Essays in Trespassing: Economics to Politics and Beyond*. Cambridge: Cambridge University Press, 1981.

―――. *Shifting Involvements: Private Interest and Public Action*. Princeton, N.J.: Princeton University Press, 1982.

Huntington, Samuel P., and Nelson, Joan M. *No Easy Choice: Political Participation in Developing Countries*. Cambridge, Mass.: Harvard University Press, 1976.

Kernell, Samuel. *Retrospective Voting and Contemporary Macrodemocracy*. Washington, D.C.: Brookings Institution, (forthcoming).

Klein, Rudolf. "Models of Man and Models of Policy: Reflections on *Exit, Voice, and Loyalty* Ten Years Later." *Milbank Memorial Fund Quarterly*, Summer 1980.

Kolarska, Lena, and Aldrich, Howard. "Exit, Voice, and Silence: Consumers' and Managers' Responses to Organizational Decline." *Organizational Studies*, 1980, no. 1.

Kuhnle, Stein. "Emigration, Democratization, and the Rise of the European Welfare States." In *Mobilization, Center-Periphery Structures, and Nation-Building* (a volume in commemoration of Stein Rokkan), edited by Per Torsvik. Bergen: Universitetsforlaget, 1981.

Laponce, Jean. "Hirschman's Voice and Exit Model as a Spatial Archetype." *Social Science Information*, 1974, no. 3.

Levin, Henry M. "Educational Choice and the Pains of Democracy." In *Public Dollars for Private Schools: The Case for Tuition Tax Credits*, edited by T. James and H. M. Levin. Philadelphia: Temple University Press, 1983.

Lorwin, Val. "Segmented Pluralism: Ideological Cleavages and Political Cohesion in the Smaller European Democracies." *Comparative Politics*, January 1971.

MacDonald, J. S. "Agricultural Organization, Migration and Labour Militancy in Rural Italy." *Economic History Review*, 1963–64, no. 1.

Michels, Roberto. *Political Parties: A Sociological Study of the Oligarchical Tendencies of Modern Democracy.* 1915. New York: Free Press, 1962.

O'Donnell, Guillermo. "On the Convergences of Hirschman's *Exit, Voice, and Loyalty* and *Shifting Involvements.*" In *Development, Democracy, and the Art of Trespassing: Essays in Honor of A. O. Hirschman,* edited by A. Foxley et al. Notre Dame, Ind.: University of Notre Dame Press, 1986.

Pizzorno, Alessandro. "Sulla razionalità della scelta democratica." *Stato e Mercato,* April 1983. English version in *Telos,* Spring 1985.

Rokkan, Stein. "Dimensions of State Formation and Nation-Building: A Possible Paradigm for Research on Variations in Europe." In *The Formation of National States in Western Europe,* edited by C. Tilly. Princeton, N.J.: Princeton University Press, 1975.

Sabel, Charles J. *Work and Politics: The Division of Labor in Industry.* Cambridge: Cambridge University Press, 1982.

Stevens, Carl M. "Voice in Medical Care Markets: 'Consumer Participation.' " *Social Science Information,* 1974, no. 3.

Weitzman, Lenore J. *The Divorce Revolution: The Unexpected Social and Economic Consequences for Women and Children in America.* New York: Free Press, 1985.

Williamson, Oliver E. *Markets and Hierarchies: Analysis and Antitrust Implications.* New York: Free Press, 1975.

PART II

5. Rival Views of Market Society

Once upon a time, not all that long ago, the social, political, and economic order under which men and women were living was taken for granted. Among the people of those idyllic times many of course were poor, sick, or oppressed, and consequently unhappy; no doubt, others managed to feel unhappy for seemingly less cogent reasons; but most tended to attribute their unhappiness either to concrete and fortuitous happenings—ill luck, ill health, the machinations of enemies, an unjust master, lord or ruler—or to remote, general, and unchangeable causes, such as human nature or the will of God. The idea that the social order—intermediate between the fortuitous and the unchangeable—may be an important cause of human unhappiness became widespread only in the modern age, particularly in the eighteenth century. Hence Saint-Just's famous phrase: "The idea of happiness is new in Europe"—it was then novel to think that happiness could be *engineered* by changing the social order, a task he and his Jacobin companions had so confidently undertaken.

Let us note in passing that the idea of a perfectible social order arose at about the same time as that of human actions and decisions having unintended effects. The latter idea was in principle tailor-made to neutralize the former: it permitted one to argue that the best intentioned institutional changes might lead, via those unforeseen consequences or "perverse effects," to all kinds of disastrous results. But the two ideas were not immediately matched up for this purpose. In the first place, the idea of the perfectibility of the social order arose primarily in the course of the French Enlightenment, while that of the unintended consequences was a principal contribution of contemporary Scottish moralists. Also, the form that the latter idea took initially stressed the happy and socially desirable outcome of self-serving individual behavior that was traditionally thought to be reprehensible, rather than uncovering the unfortunate consequences of well-intentioned social reforms. In any event, the idea of a perfectible society was not to be nipped in the bud; to the contrary, it experienced a most vigorous development and, soon after the French Revolution, reappeared in the guise of powerful critiques of the social and economic order—capitalism—emerging at the beginning of the nineteenth century.

Here I am concerned with several such critiques and their interrelations. First I shall show the close relationship and direct contradiction between an early argument *in favor of* market society and a subsequent principal *critique* of capitalism. Next, I shall point to the contradictions between this critique and another diagnosis of the ills from which much of modern capitalist society is said to suffer. And finally the tables will be turned on this second critique by yet another set of ideas. In all three cases, there was an almost total lack of communication between the conflicting theses. Intimately related intellectual formations unfolded at great length, without ever taking cognizance of each other. Such ignoring of close kin is no doubt the price paid by ideology for the self-confidence it likes to parade.

THE *DOUX-COMMERCE* THESIS

To begin, let me briefly evoke the complex of ideas and expectations that accompanied the expansion of commerce and the development of the market from the sixteenth to the eighteenth centuries. Here I must return to a principal theme of my book *The Passions and the Interests* (1977), with the hope of placating at least partially those of my readers who complained that, while I traced ideological developments in some detail up to Adam

Smith, they were left guessing what happened next, in the age—our own—that *really* mattered to them. My book dwelt on the favorable side effects that the emerging economic system was imaginatively but confidently expected to have, with respect to both the character of citizens and the characteristics of statecraft. I stressed particularly the latter—the expectation, entertained by Montesquieu and Sir James Steuart, that the expansion of the market would restrain the arbitrary actions and excessive power plays of the sovereign, both in domestic and in international politics. Here I shall emphasize instead the expected effects of commerce on the *citizen* and *civil society*. At mid-eighteenth century it became the conventional wisdom—Rousseau of course rebelled against it—that commerce was a civilizing agent of considerable power and range. Let me again cite Montesquieu's key sentence, which he placed at the very beginning of his discussion of economic matters in the *Spirit of the Laws:* "it is almost a general rule that wherever manners are gentle [*moeurs douces*] there is commerce; and wherever there is commerce, manners are gentle." The relationship between "gentle manners" and commerce is presented as mutually reinforcing, but a few sentences later Montesquieu leaves no doubt about the predominant direction of the causal link: "Commerce . . . polishes and softens [*adoucit*] barbaric ways as we can see every day."[1]

This way of viewing the influence of expanding commerce on society was widely accepted throughout most of the eighteenth century. It is stressed in two outstanding histories of progress—then a popular genre—William Robertson's *View of the Progress of Society in Europe* (1769) and Condorcet's *Esquisse d'un tableau historique du progrès de l'esprit humain* (1793–94). Robertson repeats Montesquieu almost word by word—"Commerce . . . softens and polishes the manners of men"—and Condorcet, while elsewhere critical of Montesquieu's political ideas, also followed his lead in this area quite closely:

> Manners [*moeurs*] have become more gentle [*se sont adoucies*] . . . through the influence of the spirit of commerce and industry,

---

[1] See Montesquieu, *De l'esprit des lois*, p. 8.

those enemies of the violence and turmoil which cause wealth to flee.[2]

One of the strongest statements comes in 1792, from Thomas Paine, in *The Rights of Man,*

[Commerce] is a pacific system, operating to cordialise mankind, by rendering Nations, as well as individuals, useful to each other . . . The invention of commerce . . . is the greatest approach towards universal civilization that has yet been made by any means not immediately flowing from moral principles.[3]

What was the concrete meaning of all this *douceur,* polish, gentleness, and even cordiality? Through what precise mechanisms was expanding commerce going to have such happy effects? The eighteenth-century literature is not very communicative in this regard, perhaps because it all seemed so obvious to contemporaries. The most detailed account I have been able to find appears in a technical book on commerce by one Samuel Ricard first published in 1704, which must have been highly successful as it was reprinted repeatedly through the next eighty years.

Commerce attaches [men] one to another through mutual utility. Through commerce the moral and physical passions are superseded by interest . . . Commerce has a special character which distinguishes it from all other professions. It affects the feelings of men so strongly that it makes him who was proud and haughty suddenly turn supple, bending and serviceable. Through commerce, man learns to deliberate, to be honest, to acquire manners, to be prudent and reserved in both talk and action. Sensing the necessity to be wise and honest in order to succeed, he flees vice, or at least his demeanor exhibits decency and seriousness so as not to arouse any adverse judgement on the part of present and future acquaintances; he would not dare make a spectacle of himself for fear of damaging his credit standing and thus society may well avoid a scandal which it might otherwise have to deplore.[4]

---

[2]See Condorcet, p. 238.
[3]See Paine, p. 215.
[4]See Ricard, p. 463.

Commerce is presented as a powerful moralizing agent which brings many nonmaterial improvements to society even though a bit of hypocrisy may have to be accepted into the bargain. Similar modifications of human behavior and perhaps even of human nature were later credited to the spread of commerce and industry by David Hume and Adam Smith: the virtues they specifically mention as being enhanced or brought into the world by commerce and manufacturing are industriousness and assiduity (the opposite of indolence), frugality, punctuality, and, most important perhaps for the functioning of market society, probity.[5]

There is here, then, the insistent thought that a society where the market assumes a central position for the satisfaction of human wants will not only produce considerable new wealth because of the division of labor and consequent technical progress, but generate as a by-product, or external economy, a more "polished" human type—more honest, reliable, orderly, and disciplined, as well as more friendly and helpful, ever ready to find solutions to conflicts and a middle ground for opposed opinions. Such a type will in turn greatly facilitate the smooth functioning of the market. According to this line of reasoning, capitalism, which in its early phases led a rather shaky existence, having to contend with a host of precapitalist mentalities left behind by the feudal and other "rude and barbarous" epochs, will create, in the course of time and through the very practice of trade and industry, a set of compatible psychological attitudes and moral dispositions, that are both desirable in themselves and conducive to the further expansion of the system. And at certain epochs, the speed and vigor displayed by that expansion lent considerable plausibility to this conjecture.

THE SELF-DESTRUCTION THESIS

Whatever became of this brave eighteenth-century vision? I shall reserve this topic for later and turn now to a body of thought

---

[5]See Rosenberg, pp. 59–77.

which is far more familiar to us than the *doux-commerce* thesis—and happens to be its obverse. According to it, capitalist society, far from fostering *douceur* and other fine attitudes, exhibits a pronounced proclivity to undermining the moral foundations on which any society, including its own, must rest. I shall call this the self-destruction thesis.

This thesis has a fairly numerous ancestry among both Marxist and conservative thinkers. Moreover, a political economist who was neither has recently given it renewed prominence and sophisticated treatment. In his influential book *Social Limits to Growth,* Fred Hirsch dealt at length with what he called "The Depleting Moral Legacy" of capitalism. (This is the general heading of chaps. 8–11.) He argues that the market *undermines* the moral values that are its own essential underpinnings, values that, so he asserts, have been inherited from *preceding* socioeconomic regimes, such as the feudal order. The idea that capitalism depletes or "erodes" the moral foundation needed for its functioning is put forward in the following terms:

> The social morality that has served as an understructure for economic individualism has been a legacy of the precapitalist and preindustrial past. This legacy has diminished with time and with the corrosive contact of the active capitalist values—and more generally with the greater anonymity and greater mobility of industrial society. The system has thereby lost outside support that was previously taken for granted by the individual. As individual behavior has been increasingly directed to individual advantage, habits and instincts based on communal attitudes and objectives have lost out. The weakening of traditional social values has made predominantly capitalist economies more difficult to manage. [6]

Once again, one would like to know in more detail how the market acts on values, this time in the direction of "depletion" or "erosion," rather than *douceur.* In developing his argument Hirsch makes the following principal points:

1. The emphasis on self-interest typical of capitalism makes it more difficult to secure the collective goods and cooperation

---

[6]See Hirsch, pp. 117–18.

increasingly needed for the proper functioning of the system in its later stages (chapter 11).

2. With macromanagement, Keynesian or otherwise, assuming an important role in the functioning of the system, the macromanagers must be motivated by "the general interest" rather than by their self-interest, and the system, being based on self-interest, has no way of generating the proper motivation; to the extent such motivation does exist, it is a residue of previous value systems that are likely to "erode."

3. Social virtues such as "truth, trust, acceptance, restraint, obligation," needed for the functioning of an "individualistic, contractual economy," are grounded, to a considerable extent, in religious belief, but "the individualistic, rationalistic base of the market undermines religious support."[7]

The last point stands in particularly stark contrast to the earlier conception of commerce and of its beneficial side effects. In the first place, thinkers of the seventeenth and eighteenth centuries took it for granted that they have to make do with "man as he really is" and that meant to them with someone who has been proven to be largely impervious to religious and moralistic precepts. With this realistic-pessimistic appraisal of human nature, those thinkers proceeded to discover in "interest" a principle that could replace "love" and "charity" as the basis for a well-ordered society. Second, and most important in the present context, to the extent that society is in need of moral values such as "truth, trust, etc." for its functioning, these values were confidently expected to be *generated*, rather than eroded, by the market, its practices and incentives.

Hirsch is only the latest representative of the idea that the market and capitalism harbor self-destructive proclivities. Let us now trace it back, if only to find out whether contact was ever made between these two opposite views about the moral effects of commerce and capitalism.

The idea that capitalism as a socioeconomic order somehow carries within itself the seed of its own destruction is of course

---

[7]See Hirsch, p. 143.

a cornerstone of Marxian thought. But for Marx, this familiar metaphor related to the social and economic working of the system: some of its properties, such as the tendency to concentration of capital, the falling rate of profit, the periodic crises of over-production, would bring about, with the help of an ever-more numerous and more class-conscious and combative proletariat, the socialist revolution. Thus Marx had little need to discover a more indirect and insidious mechanism that would operate as a sort of fifth column, undermining the moral foundations of the capitalist system from within. Marx did, however, help in forging one key link in the chain of reasoning that eventually led to that conception: in the *Communist Manifesto* and other early writings, Marx and Engels make much of the way in which capitalism corrodes all traditional values and institutions such as love, family, and patriotism. Everything was passing into commerce; all social bonds were dissolved through money. This perception is by no means original with Marx. Over a century earlier it was the essence of the *conservative* reaction to the advance of market society, voiced during the 1730s in England by the opponents of Walpole and Whig rule, such as Bolingbroke and his circle. The theme was taken up again, from the early nineteenth century on, by romantic and conservative critics of the Industrial Revolution. Coleridge, for example, wrote in 1817 that the "true seat and sources" of the "existing distress" are to be found in the "Overbalance of the Commercial Spirit" in relation to "natural counter-forces" such as the "ancient feelings of rank and ancestry."[8]

This ability of capitalism to "overbalance" all traditional and "higher" values was not taken as a threat to capitalism itself, at least not right away. The opposite is the case: even though the world shaped by it was often thought to be spiritually and culturally much impoverished, capitalism was viewed as an all-conquering, irresistible force, its rise widely expected to lead to a thorough remaking of society: custom would be replaced by contract, gemeinschaft by gesellschaft, the traditional by the modern;

---

[8]See Coleridge, pp. 169–70.

all spheres of social life, from the family to the state, from traditional hierarchy to longtime cooperative arrangements, would be vitally affected. Metaphors often used to describe this action of capitalism on ancient social forms ranged from the outright "dissolving" to "erosion," "corrosion," "contamination," "penetration," and "intrusion" by what Karl Polanyi was to call the "juggernaut market."

But once capitalism was thus perceived as an unbridled force, terrifyingly successful in its relentless forward drive, the thought arose naturally enough that, like all great conquerors, it just might break its neck. Being a blind force (recall the expression "blind market forces") as well as a wild one, capitalism might corrode not only traditional society and its moral values, but even those essential to its own success and survival.

To credit capitalism with extraordinary powers of expansion, penetration, and disintegration may in fact have been an adroit ideological maneuver for intimating that it was headed for disaster. The maneuver was especially effective in an age that had turned away from the idea of progress as a leading myth and was on the contrary much taken with various myths of self-destruction, from the Nibelungen to Oedipus.[9]

The simplest model for the self-destruction of capitalism might be called, in contrast to the self-reinforcing model of *doux commerce,* the *dolce vita* scenario. The advance of capitalism requires, so this story begins, that capitalists save and lead a frugal life so that accumulation can proceed apace. However, at some ill-defined point, increases in wealth resulting from successful accumulation will tend to enervate the spirit of frugality. Demands will be made for *dolce vita,* that is, for instant, rather than delayed, gratification, and when that happens capitalist progress will grind to a halt.

The idea that successful attainment of wealth will undermine the process of wealth generation is present throughout the eighteenth century from John Wesley to Montesquieu and Adam

---

[9]On the important place the theme of self-destruction held in Richard Wagner's political and economic thought, see Rather, and Eugène.

Smith. With Max Weber's essay on *The Protestant Ethic and the Spirit of Capitalism,* reasoning along such lines became fashionable once again: any evidence that the repressive ethic, alleged to be essential for the development of capitalism, may be faltering was then interpreted as a serious threat to the system's survival. Observers as diverse as Herbert Marcuse and Daniel Bell have written in this vein, unaware, it would appear, that they were merely refurbishing a well-known, much older morality tale: how the republican virtues of sobriety, civic pride, and bravery—in ancient Rome—led to victory and conquest which brought opulence and luxury, which in turn undermined those earlier virtues and destroyed the republic and eventually the empire.

While appealing in its simple dialectic, that tale has long been discredited as an explanation of Rome's decline and fall. The attempt to account for or to predict the present or future demise of capitalism in almost identical terms richly deserves a similar fate, and that for a number of reasons. Let me just point out one: the key role in this alleged process of capitalism's rise and decline is attributed first to the generation and then to the decline of personal savings so that changes in much more strategic variables, such as corporate savings, technical innovation, and entrepreneurial skill, not to speak of cultural and institutional factors, are totally left out of account.

There are less mechanical, more sophisticated forms of the self-destruction thesis. The best known is probably the one put forward by Joseph Schumpeter in *Capitalism, Socialism and Democracy,* whose second part is entitled *Can Capitalism Survive?* Schumpeter's answer to that question was rather negative, not so much, he argued, because of insuperable economic problems encountered or generated by capitalism as because of the growing hostility capitalism meets with on the part of many strata, particularly among intellectuals. It is in the course of arguing along these lines that Schumpeter writes:

> . . . capitalism creates a critical frame of mind which, after having destroyed the moral authority of so many other institutions, in the end turns against its own; the bourgeois finds to his amazement that

the rationalist attitude does not stop at the credentials of kings and popes but goes on to attack private property and the whole scheme of bourgeois values.[10]

In comparison to the *dolce vita* scenario, this is a much more general argument on self-destruction. But is it more persuasive? Capitalism is here cast in the role of the sorcerer-apprentice who does not know how to stop a mechanism once set in motion— so it demolishes itself along with its enemies. This sort of vision may have appealed to Schumpeter, who, after all, came right out of the Viennese fin-de-siècle culture for which self-destruction had become something totally familiar, unquestioned, *selbstverständlich*. Those not steeped in that tradition might not find the argument so compelling and might timidly raise the objection that, in addition to the mechanism of self-destruction, elementary forces of reproduction and *self-preservation* also ought to be taken into account. Such forces have certainly appeared repeatedly in the history of capitalism, from the first enactments of factory legislation to the introduction of social security schemes and the experimentation with countercyclical macroeconomic policies.

Schumpeter's point is made more persuasive if it can be argued that the ideological currents unleashed by capitalism are corroding the moral foundations of capitalism *inadvertently*. In other words, if the capitalist order is somehow beholden to previous social and ideological formations to a much greater extent than is realized by the conquering bourgeoisie and their ideologues, then their demolition work will have the *incidental* result of weakening the foundation on which they themselves are sitting. This idea was developed at about the time Schumpeter wrote by a very different group of European intellectuals who had also come to the United States during the 1930s: the critical theorists of the Frankfurt School, while working in the Marxist tradition, paid considerable attention to ideology as a crucial factor in historical development. In fact, a purely idealistic account of the disasters through which Western civilization was passing at the

---

[10]See Schumpeter, p. 143.

time is given by Max Horkheimer, a leading member of the group, in wartime lectures subsequently published under the title *Eclipse of Reason*.

According to Horkheimer, the commanding position of self-interest in capitalist society and the resulting agnosticism with regard to ultimate values downgraded reason to a mere instrument that would decide about the *means* to be used for reaching arbitrarily given ends, but would have nothing to say about those ends. Previously, reason and revelation had been called upon to define the ends as well as the means of human action and reason was credited with being able to shape such guiding concepts as liberty or equality or justice. But with utilitarian philosophy and self-interest-oriented capitalist practice in the saddle, reason came to lose this power, and thus " . . . the progress of subjective reason destroyed the theoretical basis of mythological, religious, and rationalistic ideas [and yet] *civilized society has up until now been living on the residue of these ideas.*"

And Horkheimer speaks movingly of "all these cherished ideas" and values, from freedom and humanity, to "enjoyment of a flower or of the atmosphere of a room . . . that, in addition to physical force and material interest, hold society together . . . but have been *undermined* by the formalization of reason."[11]

Here, then, are some early versions of Hirsch's thesis on the "depleting moral legacy" of capitalism. It is no mystery why the idea was almost forgotten in the thirty-year interval between Schumpeter-Horkheimer and Hirsch: during that era the Western world passed through a remarkably long period of sustained growth and comparative political stability. Capitalist market society, suitably modified by Keynesianism, planning, and welfare-state reforms, seemed to have escaped from its self-destructive proclivities and to generate, once again, if not *douceur*, at least considerable confidence in its ability to solve the problems that it would encounter along its way. But the sense of pervasive crisis that had characterized the 1930s and 1940s reappeared in the 1970s, in part as an after-effect of the still poorly understood

---

[11]See Horkheimer, pp. 34, 36; my italics.

mass movements of the late 1960s and in part as an immediate reaction to contemporary shocks and disarray.

Moreover, the analytical exploration of social interaction along the logic of self-interest had by then uncovered situations, such as the Prisoners' Dilemma, in which strict allegiance to self-interest was shown to bring far-from-optimal results *unless* some exogenous norms of cooperative behavior were adhered to by the actors. Now, since human behavior, allegedly guided by self-interest, had not yet had clearly disastrous effects, it was tempting to conclude that: (a) such norms, in effect, have been adhered to tacitly; (b) they must somehow predate the market society in which self-interest alone rules; and (c) their survival is now threatened. In the circumstances, the idea that capitalism lived on time (and morals) borrowed from earlier ages surfaced naturally enough once again.

What is surprising, then, is not that these somber ideas about self-destruction arose at the more difficult and somber moments of our century, but that there was a failure to connect them with earlier, more hopeful expectations of a market society bringing forth its own moral foundation, via the generation of *douceur,* probity, trust, and so on. One reason for this lack of contact is the low profile of the *doux-commerce* thesis in the nineteenth century, after its period of self-confidence in the preceding century. Another is the transfiguration of that thesis into one in which it was hard to recognize. The story of that low profile and that transfiguration must now be told.

ECLIPSE OF THE *DOUX-COMMERCE* THESIS AFTER THE EIGHTEENTH CENTURY

The most plausible explanation for the eclipse of the *doux-commerce* thesis in the nineteenth century is that it became a victim of the Industrial Revolution. The commercial expansion of the preceding centuries had of course often been violent and had created a great deal of social and human havoc, but this violence and havoc primarily affected the societies that were the objects of European penetration in Africa, Asia, and America. With the Industrial Revolution, the havoc came home. As traditional products were subjected to competitive presssure from ever new "trinkets and baubles," as large groups of laborers were displaced, and their skills became obsolete, and as all classes of society were seized by a sudden passion for enrichment, it was widely felt that a new revolutionary force had arisen in the very center of capitalist expansion.

As I have noted, that force was often characterized as wild, blind, relentless, unbridled—anything but *doux*. Only with regard to international trade was it still asserted from time to time, usually as an afterthought, that expanding transactions would bring, not only mutual material gains, but also some fine byproducts in the cultural and moral realms, such as intellectual cross-fertilization and mutual understanding and peace.[12] Within the boundaries of the nation, the expansion of industry and commerce was widely viewed as contributing to the breakdown of traditional communities, and to the loosening and disintegration of social and affective ties, rather than to their consolidation.

To be sure, here and there one can still find echoes of the older idea that civil society is largely held together by the dense network of mutual relations and obligations arising from the market and from its expansion, which in turn is fueled by an increasingly fine division of labor. In fact, as soon as the matter is put this way one's thoughts travel to Emile Durkheim and his *Division of Labor in Society*. Durkheim argued, at least in part, that the advanced division of labor in modern society functions as a substitute for the "common consciousness" that so effectively bonded more primitive societies: "it is principally [the division of

---

[12]For example, John Stuart Mill writes in *Principles of Political Economy:* "It is hardly possible to overrate the value, in the present low state of human improvement, of placing human beings in contact with persons dissimilar to themselves, and with modes of thought and action unlike those with which they are familiar . . . Such communication has always been, and is peculiarly in the present age, one of the primary sources of progress." (Collected Works, Vol. 3, p. 594)

labor] which holds together social aggregates of the higher type."
But in Durkheim's subtle thought, the transactions arising from
the division of labor were not by themselves capable of this
substitution. The decisive role was played by the many often
unintended ties that people take on or fall into in the wake of
market transactions and contractual commitments. Here are
some formulations of this thought that recur throughout the
book:

> We cooperate because we wanted to do so, but our voluntary coop-
> eration creates duties which we did not intend to assume. . . .
>
> The members [of societies with a fine division of labor] are united
> by ties that go well beyond the ever so brief moments during which
> exchange actually takes place . . . Because we exercise this or that
> domestic or social function, we are caught in a network of obligations
> which we do not have the right to forsake. . . .
>
> If the division of labor produces solidarity, this is not only because
> it makes of each person an exchanger [*échangiste*] to speak the lan-
> guage of the economists; it is because the division of labor creates
> among men a comprehensive system of rights and duties which tie
> them to one another in a durable fashion.[13]

So Durkheim's construction is a great deal more complex and
roundabout than Montesquieu's (or Sir James Steuart's): society
is *not* held together directly nor is it made peaceful and *doux* by
the network of self-interested market transactions alone; for that
sort of doctrine Durkheim has some harsh words that contrast
sharply with the seventeenth and eighteenth centuries' doctrine
about interest:

> While interest brings people closer together, this is a matter of a few
> moments only; it can only create an external tie among them . . . The
> consciences are only in superficial contact; they do not penetrate one
> another . . . every harmony of interest contains a latent or delayed
> conflict . . . for interest is what is least constant in the world.[14]

---

[13]See Durkheim, pp. 148, 192, 207, 402–3.

[14]See Durkheim, pp. 180–81. Compare this text with the exactly opposite
seventeenth- and eighteenth-century statements on the constancy and predictability of interest which I reported in *The Passions and the Interests*, pp. 48–55.

Durkheim was thus caught between the older view that interest-oriented action provides a basis for social integration and the more contemporary critique of market society as atomistic and corrosive of social cohesion. He never spelled out in concrete detail how he conceived a "solidary" society to emerge from the division of labor and eventually moved on to a more activist view that no longer counted on this mechanism to achieve social cohesion and instead stressed moral education and political action.[15] But, as I shall argue later, there may be considerable virtue in his ambivalent stance; and the idea that social bonds can be grafted onto economic transactions if conditions are favorable remains to be explored in depth.

An ambivalence similar to that of Durkheim characterized the work of his German contemporary Georg Simmel. While no one has written more powerfully on the alienating properties of money, Simmel stressed in other writings the integrating functions of various conflicts in modern society. In this connection he gave high marks to competition as an institution that fosters empathy and the building of strong social ties, not of course among the competitors but between them and an important and often overlooked third party—the customer:

The aim for which competition occurs within a society is presumably always the favor of one or more third persons. Each of the competing parties therefore tries to come as close to that third one as possible. Usually, the poisonous, divisive, destructive effects of competition are stressed and, in exchange, it is merely pointed out that it improves economic welfare. But in addition, it has, after all, this immense sociating effect. Competition compels the wooer . . . to go out to the wooed, come close to him, establish ties with him, find his strengths and weaknesses and adjust to them . . .

Innumerable times [competition] achieves what usually only love can do: the divination of the innermost wishes of the other, even before he himself becomes aware of them. Antagonistic tension with his competitor sharpens the businessman's sensitivity to the tendencies of the public, even to the point of clairvoyance, in respect to

---

[15]See Lukes, p. 178.

future changes in the public's tastes, fashion, interests . . . Modern competition is described as the fight of all against all, but at the same time it is the fight *for* all . . .

. . . In short, [competition] is a web of a thousand sociological threads by means of conscious concentration on the will and feeling and thinking of fellowmen . . . Once the narrow and naive solidarity of primitive social conditions yielded to decentralization . . . man's effort toward man, his adaptation to the other seems possible only at the price of competition, that is, of the simultaneous fight against a fellowman for a third one.[16]

Simmel's thought here comes close to that of Durkheim's, in that he also uncovers in the structure and institutions of capitalist society a functional equivalent for the simple bonds of custom and religion that (allegedly) held traditional society together. Elsewhere he shows that the advanced division of labor in modern society, and the importance of credit for the functioning of the economy, rest on, and promote, a high degree of truthfulness in social relations.[17] With his effusiveness and vivid imagery, Simmel is perhaps more successful than the austere Durkheim in convincing the reader that some features of market society make for social integration rather than the opposite.

Thus was a minority position affirmed by eminent and somewhat protean figures whose *major* contribution to social thought—through such concepts as anomie in the case of Durkheim, for example—definitely strengthened the majority view. For a counterpoint to the European sociologists' generally somber analysis of capitalism's social impact, it is tempting to look to the American scene. There we find an important group of late nineteenth- and early twentieth-century sociologists—from George Herbert Mead, Charles Cooley, and Edward Ross to the young John Dewey—who, less haunted than their European colleagues by problems of social disintegration, were simply seeking to understand how and why society coheres as well as it does. But in explaining what they called "social control," they attributed key roles to small-

---

[16]See Simmel, *Conflict and the Web of Group Affiliations*, pp. 61–63.
[17]See Simmel, *Soziologie*, pp. 260–61.

scale, face-to-face relationships, as well as to the ability of various social groups to make norms and rules effective.[18] Significantly, economic relationships are hardly ever mentioned as sources of socially integrative behavior in this literature.

This also holds true for the sociological system that Talcott Parsons later built up. In his thought, the rules of conduct that keep fraudulent behavior at bay in the marketplace derive from what he calls "collectivity-orientation," which must somehow be present in every society; he does not see such rules arising in any way out of the market itself. Given the rigid dichotomies within which the Parsonian system is conceived, there could not be much communication between market transactions, classified as "universalistic," and such "particularistic" and "diffuse" phenomena as friendship and social ties in general.[19]

So much for sociology. What about the economists? After all, they had a tradition of either outspokenly criticizing the capitalist system or defending and praising it. Should not the praisers, at least, have had an interest in keeping alive the thought that the multiple acts of buying and selling characteristic of advanced market societies forge all sorts of social ties of trust, friendliness, sociability, and thus help to hold society together? In actual fact, this sort of reasoning is conspicuously absent from professional economics literature. The reasons are several. First, economists, in their attempt to emulate, in rigor and quantitative precision, the natural sciences, had little use for the necessarily imprecise ("fuzzy") speculations about effects of economic transactions on social cohesion. Second, those trained in the tradition of classical economics had only scorn for the concern of sociologists over the more disruptive and destructive aspects of capitalism. They saw in such phenomena a short-run cost necessary to achieve superior long-run gains and were not impelled by that sort of critique of capitalism to search for or invoke any compensating positive effects which the expansion of the market might have on social life and ties.

---

[18]See Silver.
[19]See Parsons, pp. 98, 125–27.

But the principal explanation is supplied by yet another point. Economists who wish the market well have been *unable,* or rather have tied their own hands and denied themselves the opportunity, to exploit the argument about the integrative effect of markets. This is so because the argument cannot be made for the ideal market with perfect competition. The economists' claims of allocative efficiency and all-round welfare maximization are strictly valid only for this market. Involving large numbers of price-taking anonymous buyers and sellers supplied with perfect information, such markets function without any prolonged human or social contact among or between the parties. Under perfect competition there is no room for bargaining, negotiation, remonstration or mutual adjustment, and the various operators that contract together need not enter into recurrent or continuing relationships as a result of which they would get to know each other well. Clearly this latter tie-forming effect of markets can be important only when there are substantial departures or "lapses" from the ideal competitive model. But the fact is that such lapses are exceedingly frequent and important. Nonetheless, pro-market economists either have singled out ties among suppliers and, like Adam Smith, castigated them as "conspiracies against the public"; or, much more frequently, have belittled the various lapses in an attempt to present the reality of imperfect competition as coming close to the ideal. In this manner, they have endeavored to endow the market system with *economic* legitimacy. But, by the same token, they have sacrificed the *sociological* legitimacy that could rightfully have been claimed for the way, so unlike the perfect-competition model, most markets function in the real world.[20]

Only in recent years have economists developed a number of approaches that do not look at departures from the competitive model as either sinful or negligible. To the contrary, with their

---

[20]I made a similar point in *Exit, Voice, and Loyalty* (p. 22). In the same vein, Williamson has recently written about the "inhospitality tradition" of economists with regard to organizational innovations of business enterprise: such innovations were always suspected of entailing departures from the competitive model (p. 1540).

stress on transaction costs, limited information and imperfect maximization, these approaches explain and justify the widespread existence of continuing relationships between buyers and sellers, the frequent establishment of hierarchies in preference to markets partly as a result of such "relational exchange," the use of "voice" rather than "exit" to correct mutual dissatisfaction, and similar phenomena that make for meaningful tie-forming interaction between parties to transactions. The stage could thus be set for a partial rehabilitation of the *doux-commerce* thesis.

THE FEUDAL-SHACKLES THESIS

With all due respect for these new developments, it remains true that the *doux-commerce* thesis about the beneficial effects of expanding capitalism on social relations, so popular in the eighteenth century, all but disappeared from the intellectual stage during the protracted subsequent period which saw the full development of capitalist society and, concurrently, the deployment of a far more critical argument about its social impact. But the ways of ideology are intricate: upon looking closely it appears that the optimistic *doux-commerce* thesis does reemerge after all in the nineteenth and twentieth centuries, but as part and parcel of an important *critical* view of capitalist development. It is as though the thesis, faced with the widespread critical attitude toward capitalism, managed to survive by changing camp.

So far we have become acquainted with one kind of critical analysis of capitalism's impact on the social order. What I called the self-destruction thesis views capitalism as an extraordinarily powerful force that dissolves all previous social formations and ideologies and even chips away at capitalism's own moral foundations. But a very different, almost opposite, critique has also been prominently voiced: here the real grudge against capitalism and its standard-bearer, the bourgeoisie, is their *weakness* vis-à-vis traditional social forces, their unwillingness to stage a frontal attack, and often their submissiveness and "spineless" subservience toward the well-entrenched aristocrats of the ancien régime. As in the case of the self-destruction thesis, this is not a unified theory, but a series of contributions from different authors, for different purposes, and in different contexts. Nevertheless, there is a common theme: a number of societies that have been penetrated by capitalism are criticized and considered to be in trouble because this penetration has been too partial, timid, and halfhearted, with substantial elements of the previous social order being left intact. These elements are referred to variously as feudal overhang, shackles, remnants, residues, ballast, or relics and they turn out to retain considerable influence and power. Inasmuch as the societies in question are criticized for not having liquidated this feudal overhang, it has also often been said of them that they have "failed to complete the bourgeois revolution." In short, this group of ideas can be referred to as the feudal-shackles or unfinished-bourgeois-revolution thesis.

While the feudal-shackles thesis is clearly opposed to the self-destruction thesis, it is but an inverted version of the *doux-commerce* thesis. This is not hard to see. Things would have worked out famously, so the feudal-shackles thesis asserts implicitly, *if only* commerce, the market, capitalism had been able to unfold freely, if only they had not been reined in by precapitalist institutions and attitudes. The civilizing work of the market might be done either directly, according to the original script of the *doux-commerce* thesis, or indirectly, by opening the way to the proletarian revolution and to fraternal socialism, after the rapid sweep of capitalism. Here the *douceur* brought by the market would come at one remove. But, alas, neither one nor the other of these happy outcomes was to materialize as hostile forces of bygone social formations retained unexpected strength. The feudal-shackles thesis thus rests on the *doux-commerce* thesis—without, of course, acknowledging the affiliation. It *is* the *doux-commerce* thesis in negative disguise, in critical garb, stood on its head.

We now have two major critiques of capitalism, the self-destruction and the feudal-shackles theses. Each points to some "contradictions" of capitalism, but it is already apparent that the two views also violently contradict one another.

There is here then a contradiction between contradictions,

or, to borrow a mathematical term, a second-order contradiction of capitalism. The nature of this contradiction will become clearer as the historical development and the various shapes of the feudal-shackles thesis are reviewed briefly.

However contradictory, the two theses can both be traced—as might be expected: after all, they are both critiques of capitalism—to the writings of Karl Marx. That he prepared the ground for the self-destruction thesis because of his emphasis on the all-corrosive properties of capitalism has already been noted. Similarly, the feudal-shackles thesis is adumbrated in Marx when he writes in the preface of *Capital* that in comparison to England the Germans suffer not only from all the modern woes of capitalist expansion, but from a "long series of inherited afflictions, resulting from the persistence of antiquated modes of production that have outlived their usefulness, with their sequel of adverse social and political relations."[21]

From this kind of observation it is not a big jump to assert that the persistence and unexpected strength of precapitalist forms, together with the correlative *weakness* of capitalist structures, could become a major problem in certain societies. In which ones? The German example suggests that it might be in those where capitalist development is delayed, the delay being precisely due to the resilience of precapitalist forms, to the fact that the feudal "cobwebs" have not been neatly "swept away" by a thoroughgoing "bourgeois revolution." On the contrary, so the story goes, the indigenous bourgeoisie in such countries was not only weak but servile, supine, craven, wishing to make it within the old order and submissive to its code and values. This results in the "distortion" or "stunting" of capitalist structures. In other words, the trouble with capitalism, suddenly, is not that it is so strong as to be self-destructing but that it is too weak to play the "progressive" role history has supposedly assigned to it.

The fullest development of these ideas has occurred in our time with some neo-Marxist analyses of the countries of the capitalist periphery. But there are earlier important applications, and

---

[21]See Marx, p. 7.

Schumpeter's well-known theory of imperialism is a case in point. As already noted, one of the fondest hopes expressed in the seed-time of capitalist development was that worldwide trade and investment consequent upon capitalist development would make war impossible and lay a solid foundation for peace and friendship among nations. When, around the beginning of the twentieth century, the illusory nature of this hope became only too obvious, it was attractive to argue, along exactly opposite lines, that capitalism itself inevitably leads to great-power rivalry and war. This, with some variants, was indeed affirmed by the economic theories of imperialism proposed around that time by J. A. Hobson, Rosa Luxemburg, Rudolf Hilferding, and Lenin. But Schumpeter, writing during World War I, came to the rescue of the earlier optimistic view by arguing that capitalism, in and of itself, could lead only to peace. To him, the rational, calculating spirit of capitalism was wholly incompatible with the reckless gambling characteristic of warmaking in the modern age or any age. What had gone wrong? Precisely that capitalism had not proven vigorous enough, had not been able to alter decisively either the social structure or the mentality of the precapitalist age with its disaster-bound addiction to heroic antics.

Strangely enough, Schumpeter therefore became an articulate spokesman—far more so than Marx—both for the feudal-shackles thesis, according to which the trouble with capitalism was its *weakness* (vis-à-vis precapitalist forms), and for the self-destruction thesis which emphasizes capitalism's corrosive strength. To explain this apparent inconsistency, it must first be pointed out that the texts containing the two theses were written more than twenty years apart from one another. Second, the two theses, in spite of their contradiction, have various characteristics in common: both underline the importance of ideology and mentality and thereby are self-consciously critical of Marxism; and both take an obvious pleasure in stressing the key role of the irrational in human affairs, once again in line with the contemporary intellectual climate due to such figures as Freud, Bergson, Sorel, and Pareto.

In the meantime, however, the Marxists were also picking

up the hints dropped by the master. Naturally enough, when they criticized the experience of certain countries under capitalism for lack of dynamism, they stressed structural rather than ideological factors. In Italy, for example, Antonio Gramsci and Emilio Sereni analyzed the Risorgimento as an "incomplete" or "failed" bourgeois revolution because political unification in the second half of the nineteenth century was not accompanied by agrarian reform or revolution, The weakness of the Italian bourgeoisie and its lack of Jacobin energies were thus proclaimed as the aboriginal flaw, or *vizio d'origine,* of modern Italian history, the root cause of all subsequent woes, from weak economic development to the advent of Fascism.[22]

Some of this analysis at least was later controverted by economic historians who pointed out that the so-called "failure to complete the bourgeois revolution" by land reform actually permitted capital accumulation to proceed in the north. So the alleged failure had its positive side in that it made possible the vigorous industrial push that did take place in the country's north prior to World War I.[23]

But to return to the failed or incomplete-revolution thesis: In Italy, the principal objective pursued by leaders of the Risorgimento was national unification and it was accomplished. To characterize that movement as a failed bourgeois revolution therefore amounted to *inventing* a failure by substituting some imaginary telos or historical geist for the real intentions of human agents. In nineteenth-century Germany, on the other hand, the failures of the political movements of 1848 were all too real, and they did expose the political weakness of the German bourgeois liberals. These events lent themselves to a straightforward interpretation, along feudal-remnants lines. "It is the tragedy of the bourgeoisie that it has not yet defeated its predecessor, that is, feudalism, when its new enemy, the proletariat, has already appeared on the stage of history." Clearly, this elegant formulation of Georg

---

[22]A collection of articles around the concept, fortunately critical for the most part, is in *Il vizio d'origine.*

[23]See Romeo, and Gerschenkron, chapter 5.

Lukács applied particularly to Germany and Central Europe, where the battle with the bourgeoisie's alleged historical "predecessors," the aristocratic and military power-holders, was never really joined. After some skirmishes, circa 1848, the bourgeoisie was ready for a compromise with the powerful "feudal remnants" and it is this compromise, according to numerous observers, which deserves much of the blame for the disasters of modern German history.

In spite of the historical importance of the Italian and German cases, the notion that the bourgeois class, which emerges with the rise of commerce and industry, does not necessarily sweep away all precapitalist formations had to be rediscovered, with great fanfare, again and again. This was so, for example, in Latin America. During the growth years following World War II, social scientists looking at the "periphery" generally set out with the unspoken assumption that capitalism was (and always has been) performing faultlessly in the center; hence, so they concluded, the difficulties of the periphery must be due to some deviation from the pattern the center had followed. Within this conceptual framework the feudal-shackles thesis—or close analogues—provided an appealing explanation.

Coining an expressive and successful metaphor, the political scientist Charles Anderson described the Latin American social and political scene as a " 'living museum' in which all the forms of political authority of Western historic experience continue to exist and operate," implying that in the West these forms followed one another in an orderly sequence.[24]

Latin American societies, it was concluded, somehow did not manage to extirpate superannuated relations of production and this was why they were in trouble. Once more the culprit was the weakness of the indigenous bourgeoisie, ever ready to sell out to the old landowning elites or to foreign investors and preferably to both. Such was the essence of much neo-Marxist analysis, which, this time, did not bother to blame the bourgeoisie for not playing its "historic role." Rather, it was now denied that,

---

[24]I am not denying, *of course,* that industrialization in Latin America had characteristics of its own; in fact, I have tried to set them forth in some detail.

given the peripheral position of Latin American societies, their bourgeoisie could ever come to play any constructive developmental role at all; this congenital incapacity was meant to be conveyed by the coining of insulting terms such as *"comprador bourgeoisie"* (Paul Baran) and *"lumpenbourgeoisie"* (Andre Gunder Frank). Quite consistently with this position, what industrialization and capitalist development have taken place in Latin America and elsewhere in the periphery were systematically belittled and berated.

This is not the place to discuss the truth value of these conceptions and assertions except to state that I have my doubts and have expressed them elsewhere.[25] I must go on and call attention to a strange turn taken quite recently by the feudal-shackles theorists.

Until now it always served to explain why one particular backward or latecoming country's economic development was experiencing difficulties *in comparison to* a leading country or countries, where development was believed to have proceeded smoothly and vigorously. Now, suddenly, a number of people are telling us that, at least in Europe, no such blessed country ever existed and that the bourgeoisie was weak, craven, and spineless all along. The strongest assertion of this sort is made in *The Persistence of the Ancien Régime* by Arno Mayer. According to him, the situation in all of Europe was, at least until World War I, very much like what it has been alleged to be today in the Latin American periphery: capitalist development was anything but dynamic and penetrative, the bourgeoisie was everywhere subservient to the established nobility, and the elites of the ancien régime retained not only economic and political power, but cultural hegemony as well. And, in a light variant of the Schumpeter thesis on imperialism, Mayer attributes the outbreak of World War I to the reaction of these traditional power-holders, when they perceived for the first time some distant rumblings of troubles for their hitherto uncontested dominion.

This near universalization of the feudal-remnants thesis rep-

---

[25]See Hirschman, Albert O., *A Bias for Hope*, chapter 3.

resented a particularly surprising and daring proposition for England and France, the two major countries where, so it had long been thought, total victories had been achieved by the bourgeoisie and capitalism as a result of political revolution in France and industrial revolution in England. Now, it must be noted that this questioning of the status of France and England as model countries occurred when the golden "growth years" of the 1950s and 1960s were definitely behind us and new questions were being asked about the health of capitalist economy and society. In fact, Mayer's book, with its generalization of the feudal-shackles thesis to countries hitherto outside its reach, does not stand alone. According to a related volume by Martin Wiener on England, that country's industrial spirit had only the briefest flowering circa 1850 and from then on was in eclipse as middle-class intellectuals imbued with gentry ideals staged a successful counterrevolution of values.[26] Carrying this genre to extremes—and becoming a succès de scandale in the process—is *L'idéologie française* by Bernard-Henri Lévy. According to this author, French social and political thought was dominated, from the mid-nineteenth century to World War II and from one end to the other of the ideological spectrum, by a repulsive amalgam of racist and protofascist drivel!

My purpose here is not to criticize these works, but to show how the feudal-shackles thesis has lately been applied to countries, such as England and France, that had been almost by definition excluded from it. The reason is, of course, that the most advanced capitalist countries were generally thought to be suffering from contradictions that arose from capitalism's strength, rather than from its weakness.

In sum, the generalization of the feudal-shackles thesis pulls out two rugs simultaneously: one from under common conceptions about the specific nature and problems of capitalism in the periphery (and among European latecomers); and the other from under the self-destruction thesis, whose favorite terrain

---

[26]An early argument on the historical weakness of the English bourgeoisie is in Anderson, Perry, "Origins of the Present Crisis."

must surely be found, if anywhere, in the most advanced countries.

AMERICA, OR THE PERILS OF NOT HAVING A FEUDAL PAST

To get over our puzzlement and to complete our pageant of theories, it will be helpful, at this point, to turn to the United States, a preeminent outpost of capitalism that has remained unmentioned up to now. The reason is that this country alone has escaped from the generalization of the feudal-shackles thesis. No one has yet argued that the United States is or has ever been in the grip of some ancien régime or that its capitalist development has been hampered and distorted by tenacious gentlemanly values or entrenched feudal institutions except for the South and slavery. Rather, the United States has generally been taken to be the confirmation *a contrario* of the feudal-shackles thesis: its vigorous capitalist development, combined with sturdy political pluralism, has often been attributed precisely to the absence of a feudal background. This idea that the United States is uniquely blessed because, unlike old Europe, it is not weighed down by the shackles of the past was expressed as early as 1818 by Goethe in the poem "To the United States," whose opening lines read:

Amerika, Du hast es besser
Als unser Kontinent, der Alte,
Hast keine verfallenen Schlösser . . . [27]

Tocqueville gave this same comparative appraisal its classic expression, of course, with the single, oft-quoted sentence: "The great advantage of the Americans is that they have come to democracy without having to endure democratic revolutions; and

---

[27]"America, you are better off / Than our old continent / You have no castles in ruins . . . "

that they are born equal, instead of becoming so."[28] Many American commentators have been eager and happy to make these flattering insights their own. Thus arose what has become known as the thesis of "American exceptionalism," which holds that America is exceptionally fortunate among nations because of its peculiar historical background (plus a few other factors, such as abundant natural resources and size) and is therefore free from the unending internal conflicts of other Western countries.

But now comes a surprise, even a *coup de théâtre*. A major contributor to this literature is Louis Hartz with his classic *The Liberal Tradition in America*. Hartz fully accepts the idea that the United States is uniquely exempt from feudal relics. He duly cites Goethe's poem and even uses the Tocquevillian sentence as his epigraph. Yet, upon reading the book with some attention, one notices something that he never tells you outright: namely, he is in intimate disagreement with both Goethe and Tocqueville! His book is, in effect, a long lament about the many *evils* that have befallen the United States because of the *absence* of feudal remnants, relics, and the like. Throughout, this vaunted absence is shown to be a mixed blessing at best, and is most frequently depicted as a poisoned gift or a *curse* in disguise.

Hartz's reasoning is basically very simple—this is why it is so powerful. Having been "born equal," without any sustained struggle against the "father"—that is, the feudal past—America is deprived of what Europe has in abundance: social and ideological diversity. *But such diversity is one of the prime constituents of genuine liberty.* According to Hartz, the lack of ideological diversity in America has meant the absence of an authentic conservative tradition, is responsible for the often noted weaknesses of socialist movements, and has even made for the protracted sterility of liberal political thought itself. What is still more serious, this lack of diversity stimulates the ever-present tendencies to-

---

[28]Tocqueville, vol. 2, p. 108. This sentence concludes a short chapter entitled "How it comes about that individualism is stronger after a democratic revolution than at other times" where Tocqueville lists the many conflicts and problems afflicting societies, such as the French, that have had to "suffer a democratic revolution."

ward a "tyranny of the majority" inspired by America's "irrational Lockianism" or its "colossal liberal absolutism."[29]

This state of affairs is shown to have numerous implications, mostly deplorable, in both domestic and international affairs. I shall cite only one observation, because of its relevance to present-day events. Analyzing the New Deal and its considerable departures from the traditional liberal credo, Hartz notes that Roosevelt put across his innovative reforms as an exercise in "pragmatism" and in "bold and persistent experimentation": " . . . the crucial thing was that, lacking the socialist challenge and of course the old corporate challenge on the right such as the European conservatisms still embodied, he did not need to spell out any real philosophy at all."[30]

According to Hartz, Roosevelt owed much of his success to this manner of presenting his policies as just a "sublimated 'Americanism.' " Today, of course, we can appreciate the high cost of the maneuver. The New Deal reforms, as well as the welfare-state schemes that were added later, were never truly consolidated as an integral part of a new economic order or ideology. Unlike similar policies in other economically advanced countries, these reforms failed to achieve full legitimacy and remained vulnerable, as is currently evident, to attack from revivalist forces adhering strictly to the aboriginal "colossal liberal absolutism."

Hartz's analysis achieved or permitted substantial insights by reversing the conventional lament about the presence and influence of feudal remnants in capitalist societies. He shows that other, perhaps no less troublesome, kinds of difficulties can plague a nation, just *because* it is in the "enviable," "exceptional" situation of not having a feudal past. Hartz's position, I should add, has been strengthened and extended by recent macrosociological speculations that tend to view feudal society, with its complex institutional structure and built-in conflicts, as the indispensable

---

[29]Hartz, pp. 140–42, 11, 285.
[30]See Hartz, p. 263

seedbed of both Western democracy and capitalist development.[31] Conversely, Claudio Véliz's essay on Latin America argues, very much in the spirit of Louis Hartz, that the lack of genuine feudal structures in that continent's historical experience accounts for its "centralist tradition," which in turn is held to be responsible for its principal troubles.

TOWARD A *TABLEAU IDÉOLOGIQUE*

The focus of my extended tour d'horizon of interpretations of capitalist development has been not on what is right or wrong with capitalism (from the points of view of justice, efficiency, or growth), but on what *goes* right or wrong; that is, on ideas about the likely economic and noneconomic (moral, social, political) dynamics of the system. In case the reader feels bewildered by the seeming jumble of theses that I have paraded, I shall now demonstrate, by a two-by-two table, that the structure of my argument has really been quite simple as well as beautifully symmetrical.

I have essentially dealt with four types of theses or theories and have presented them in a sequence such that each successive thesis is in some respect the negation of the preceding one. According to the *doux-commerce* thesis of the eighteenth century, with which I started out, the market and capitalism were going to create a moral environment in which a good society as well as the market itself were bound to flourish. But soon there arose, in counterpoint, the self-destruction thesis, which asserts that, to the contrary, the market, with its vehement emphasis on individual self-interest, corrodes all traditional values, including those on the basis of which the market itself is functioning. Next, the feudal-shackles thesis demonstrates instead how capitalism

---

[31]For converging analyses along these lines, it is possible to cite the works of two authors with very different ideological positions: *Les origines du capitalisme* by Baechler, and *Lineages of the Absolutist State* by Perry Anderson.

Dominance of Market vs. Influential Persistence of Precapitalist Forms: Their Effects on Market Society

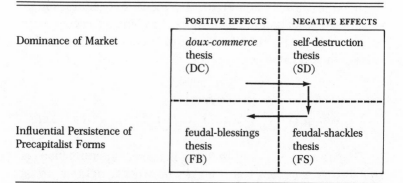

	POSITIVE EFFECTS	NEGATIVE EFFECTS
Dominance of Market	*doux-commerce* thesis (DC)	self-destruction thesis (SD)
Influential Persistence of Precapitalist Forms	feudal-blessings thesis (FB)	feudal-shackles thesis (FS)

is coming to grief, not because of its own excessive energies, but because of powerful residues of precapitalist values and institutions. This thesis is in turn contradicted by the demonstration that calamitous results follow from the *absence* of a feudal past. This is the thesis of Louis Hartz, which can also be called the *feudal-blessings thesis*, as it implies that a feudal background is a *favorable* factor for subsequent democratic-capitalist development. Thus we end up with a position that is in obvious conflict with the initial *doux-commerce* thesis; for, in the latter, the market and self-interested behavior are viewed as a benign force that is in fact destined to emancipate civil society from "feudal shackles."

A schematic presentation or mapping makes it easy to perceive the relationship between these theses. It promotes a principal aim of this essay, which has been to establish contact between a number of ideological formations that are in fact closely related but have evolved in total isolation from one another. Rather wondrously, the various ideologies, even though secreted in such isolation, end up composing a complete pattern, as shown in the table; it is as though four blindfolded children did a perfect job jointly coloring a coloring book.

So far I have essentially been, or pretended to be, a spectator and chronicler of that considerable portion of the Human Comedy which is involved with the production of ideologies. Faced with the highly diverse views here outlined, I confess, however, to a moderate interest in the question as to which one is *right*. And here the simple *tableau idéologique* I have presented can also be of use. First of all, it suggests that, however incompatible the various theories may be, each might still have its "hour of truth" and/or its "country of truth" as it applies in a given country or group of countries during some stretch of time. This is actually how these theses arose, for all of them were fashioned with a specific country or group of countries in mind.

But the table is especially useful if one wishes to pursue a more complex (and, I think, more adequate) way of giving each contending view its due. It is conceivable that, even at one and the same point in space and time, a simple thesis holds only a portion of the full truth and needs to be complemented by one or several of the others, however incompatible they may look at first sight. The table then invites us to try out systematically the various possible combinations of the four theses. In the following, I shall limit this exercise to the three "contradictions" with which we are already familiar.[32] But now the task is to explore whether it is at all possible and useful to combine the theses that constitute those contradictions.

Clearly there are degrees of incompatibility among points of

---

[32]Given the four theses, there are altogether six such pairwise combinations and we already know that four of them are "full of contradictions." The remaining two, that is, the diagonal pairs DC-FS and SD-FB, should be nicely compatible as, say, the *doux-commerce* thesis is here coupled with the negation of its negation. This is indeed the case. I pointed out that the feudal-shackles thesis could be understood as the *doux-commerce* thesis in disguise. To combine these two theses therefore does not really yield new information or interpretation.

If we look at the other diagonal pair, the self-destruction and the feudal-blessings theses, a similar conclusion follows. In Hartz's argument about the dire consequences of the lack of a feudal past, there is implicit a concern that a society wholly dominated by the market would face considerable dangers. The two theses are eminently compatible and to bring them together does not add much to either one or the other.

I shall not deal in the text with the DC-FB pair. These two do add up to a real contradiction, for they are two very different accounts of the reasons for capitalism's health and strength. But, in this manner, the pair is little more than the mirror image of the SD-FS pair with its two contrasting accounts of the difficulties encountered by market society. I discuss this latter pair in the text, along with the remaining two pairs, DC-SD and FS-FB.

view or doctrines that are contradictory on the face of it. As already noted, a highly irreconcilable contradiction is that between the self-destruction thesis and the feudal-shackles thesis. The former views capitalism as a wild, unbridled force which, having swept away everything in its path, finally does itself in by successfully attacking its own foundations. The feudal-shackles thesis, on the other hand, sees capitalists as weak and subservient and easily overpowered, distracted, or distorted by precapitalist forms and values: a determined eclectic or lover of reconciliations could still argue that capitalism has the knack of doing away with all in its "legacy" that is good and functional (that is, with such values as truth and honesty, not to speak of *gemütlichkeit*) while leaving intact, and utterly succumbing to, all in precapitalist society that is pernicious. But is it conceivable that any historical formation would have such an unerring, schlemiel-like instinct for going wrong?

Here, then, is our most genuine, most irreducible "second-order contradiction." It remains possible, of course, that each of these accounts—the self-destruction and the feudal-remnants theses—is valuable in explaining the difficulties capitalism is experiencing in different settings. In other words, I do not wish to intimate that these two theses checkmate each other, so that we can happily conclude that capitalism is wholly exempt from trouble on account of either of them.

By now, however, we know that these two accounts are contradicted not only by each other but also by points of view that evaluate as *positive* the very factors these accounts view negatively. I am referring to the *doux-commerce* and the feudal-blessings theses, which will now be brought into play.

Take, first, the feudal-shackles and the feudal-blessings theses. As soon as we examine the likelihood that both may be true at the same time, it becomes obvious that nothing stands in the way of that sort of amalgam, which, on the contrary, seems immediately *more* probable than the eventuality that just one of the theses holds to the total exclusion of the other. Mixing the two means that precapitalist forms and values hamper the full development of capitalism while also bequeathing something precious to it. A mature appraisal surely needs to be aware of both lines of influence, and the balance is likely to be different in each concrete historical situation.

This conclusion applies even more to our last remaining pair: the *doux-commerce* and self-destruction theses. Once one inquires whether both these theses could hold at the same time it becomes obvious that this is not only possible but overwhelmingly likely. For capitalism to be both self-reinforcing and self-undermining is not any more "contradictory" than for a business firm to have income and outgo at the same time! Insofar as social cohesion is concerned, for example, the constant practice of commercial transactions generates feelings of trust, empathy for others, and similar *doux* feelings; but on the other hand, as Montesquieu already knew, such practice permeates all spheres of life with the element of calculation and of instrumental reason. Once this view is adopted, the moral basis of capitalist society will be seen as being constantly depleted and replenished at the same time. An excess of depletion over replenishment and a consequent crisis of the system is then, of course, possible, but the special circumstances making for it would have to be noted, just as it might be possible to specify conditions under which the system would gain in cohesion and legitimacy.

It is now becoming clear why, in spite of our lip service to the dialectic, we find it so hard to acknowledge that contradictory processes might actually be at work in society. It is not just a question of difficulty of perception, but one of considerable psychological resistance and reluctance: to accept that the *doux-commerce* and the self-destruction theses (or the feudal-shackles and feudal-blessings theses) might *both* be right makes it much more difficult for the social observer, critic, or "scientist" to impress the general public by proclaiming some inevitable outcome of current processes.

But after so many failed prophecies, is it not in the interest of social science to embrace complexity, be it at some sacrifice of its claim to predictive power?

Bibliographical References

Anderson, Charles W. *Politics and Economic Change in Latin America*. Princeton, N.J.: Van Nostrand, 1967.

Anderson, Perry. "Origins of the Present Crisis," *New Left Review* (January–February 1964): 26–53.

———. *Lineages of the Absolutist State*. London: NLB, 1974.

Baechler, Jean. *Les origines du capitalisme*. Paris: Gallimard, 1974.

Baker, Keith Michael. *Condorcet: From Natural Philosophy to Social Mathematics*. Chicago, Ill.: Chicago University Press, 1975.

Bell, Daniel. *The Cultural Contradictions of Capitalism*. New York: Basic Books, 1976.

Benjamin, Walter. *Deutsche Menschen*. Frankfurt: Suhrkamp, 1962.

Coleridge, Samuel Taylor. *Collected Works*. Vol. 6, *Lay Sermons*. London: Routledge and Kegan Paul; Princeton, N.J.: Princeton University Press, 1972.

Condorcet, Marquis de. *Esquisse d'un tableau historique du progrès de l'esprit humain*. Paris, 1795.

Durkheim, Émile. *De la division du travail social*. 1893. Paris: F. Alcan, 1902.

Eugène, Eric. *Les idées politiques de Richard Wagner*. Paris: Publications Universitaires, 1973.

Gerschenkron, Alexander. *Economic Backwardness in Historical Perspective*. Cambridge, Mass.: Harvard University Press, 1962.

Gramsci, Antonio. *Il risorgimento*. Turin: G. Einaudi, 1949.

Hartz, Louis. *The Liberal Tradition in America*. New York: Harcourt, Brace, 1955.

Hirsch, Fred. *Social Limits to Growth*. Cambridge, Mass., and London: Harvard University Press, 1976.

Hirschman, Albert O. *Exit, Voice, and Loyalty: Responses to Decline in Firms, Organizations, and States*. Cambridge, Mass.: Harvard University Press, 1970.

———. *A Bias for Hope: Essays on Development and Latin America*. New Haven, Conn.: Yale University Press, 1971.

———. *The Passions and the Interests: Political Arguments for Capitalism before Its Triumph*. Princeton, N.J.: Princeton University Press, 1977.

———. *Essays in Trespassing: Economics to Politics and Beyond*. Cambridge: Cambridge University Press, 1981.

Horkheimer, Max. *Eclipse of Reason*. New York: Oxford University Press, 1947.

Lévy, Bernard-Henri. *L'idéologie française*. Paris: Bernard Grasset, 1981.

Lukács, Georg. *Geschichte und Klassenbewusstsein*. Neuwied, Germany: Luchterhand, 1968.

Lukes, Steven. *Emile Durkheim: His Life and Work*. New York: Harper and Row, 1972.

Marcuse, Herbert. "Industrialization and Capitalism." *New Left Review* (March–April 1965): 3–17.

Marx, Karl. *Das Kapital*. 1872. Vienna and Berlin: Verlag für Literatur und Politik, 1932.

Mayer, Arno. *The Persistence of the Ancien Régime*. New York: Pantheon Books, 1981.

Mill, John Stuart. *Principles of Political Economy.* 1848. Vols. 2, 3 of *Collected Works.* Toronto: University of Toronto Press, 1965.

Montesquieu, Charles Louis. *De l'esprit des lois.* 1748. Paris: Garnier, 1961.

Paine, Thomas. *The Rights of Man.* 1792. New York: E. P. Dutton, 1951.

Parsons, Talcott. *The Social System.* Glencoe, Ill.: Free Press, 1951.

Rather, L. J. *The Dream of Self-Destruction: Wagner's Ring and the Modern World.* Baton Rouge: Louisiana State University Press, 1979.

Ricard, Samuel. *Traité général du commerce.* Amsterdam: Chez E. van Harrevelt et Soeters, 1781.

Robertson, William. *View of the Progress of Society in Europe.* 1769. Edited by Felix Gilbert. Chicago, Ill.: Chicago University Press, 1972.

Romeo, Rosario. *Risorgimento e capitalismo.* Bari, Italy: Laterza, 1959.

Rosenberg, Nathan. "Neglected Dimensions in the Analysis of Economic Change." *Oxford Bulletin of Economics and Statistics* 26, no. 1 (1964): 59–77.

Schumpeter, Joseph A. *Capitalism, Socialism and Democracy.* New York: Harper, 1942.

———."The Sociology of Imperialisms." *Imperialism and Social Classes.* 1917. Edited by Paul Sweezy. New York: Kelley, 1951.

Sereni, Emilio. *Il capitalismo nelle campagne. 1860–1900.* Turin: G. Einaudi, 1947.

Silver, Allan. "Small Worlds and the Great Society: The Social Production of Moral Order." MS, 1980.

Simmel, Georg. *Soziologie.* 1908. Leipzig: Duncker and Humblot, 1923.

———. *Conflict and the Web of Group Affiliations.* Translated by Kurt H. Wolff. Glencoe, Ill.: Free Press, 1955.

Smith, Adam. *The Wealth of Nations.* 1776. New York: Modern Library Edition, 1937.

Tocqueville, Alexis de. *De la démocratie en Amérique.* 1840. Paris: Gallimard, 1961.

Véliz, Claudio. *The Centralist Tradition of Latin America.* Princeton, N.J.: Princeton University Press, 1980.

Il vizio d'origine. Biblioteca della Libertá. Florence, Italy, April-September 1980.

Weber, Max. *The Protestant Ethic and the Spirit of Capitalism.* 1904–5. New York: Scribner's, 1958.

Wiener, Martin J. *English Culture and the Decline of the Industrial Spirit, 1850–1980.* Cambridge: Cambridge University Press, 1981.

Williamson, Oliver E. "The Modern Corporation: Origins, Evolution, Attributes." *Journal of Economic Literature* (December 1981): 1537–68.

6. *Against Parsimony:*

THREE EASY WAYS
OF COMPLICATING
SOME CATEGORIES OF
ECONOMIC DISCOURSE

Economics as a science of human behavior has been grounded in a remarkably parsimonious postulate: that of the self-interested, isolated individual who chooses freely and rationally among alternative courses of action after computing their prospective costs and benefits. In recent decades, a group of economists has shown considerable industry and ingenuity in applying this way of interpreting the social world to a series of ostensibly noneconomic phenomena, from crime to the family, and from collective action to democracy. The "economic" or "rational-actor" approach has yielded some important insights, but its onward sweep has also revealed some of its intrinsic weaknesses. As a result, it has become possible to mount a critique which, ironically, can be carried all the way back to the heartland of the would-be conquering discipline. That the economic approach presents us with too simpleminded an account of even such fundamental economic processes as consumption and production is my basic thesis here.

I am not alone in this view. Schelling has noted that "the human mind is something of an embarrassment to certain disciplines, notably economics . . . that have found the model of the rational consumer to be powerfully productive." And in a well-known article, significantly entitled "Rational Fools: A Critique of the Behavioral Foundations of Economic Theory," Sen has asserted not long ago that "traditional [economic] theory has *too little* structure."[1] Noting that individual preferences and actual choice behavior are far from being always identical, he introduced novel concepts, such as commitment and second-order preferences. Like any virtue, so he seemed to say, parsimony in theory construction can be overdone, and something is sometimes to be gained by making things more complicated. I have increasingly come to feel this way. Some years ago, I suggested that criticism from customers, or "voice," should be recognized as a force keeping management of firms and organizations on their toes, along with competition or "exit," and it took a book to cope with the resulting complications. Here I deal with various other realms of economic inquiry that stand similarly in need of being rendered more complex. In concluding, I examine whether the various complications have some element in common: that would in turn simplify and unify matters.

TWO KINDS OF PREFERENCE CHANGES

A fruitful distinction has been made, by Sen and others, between first-order and second-order preferences, or between preferences and metapreferences, respectively. I shall use the latter terminology here. Economics has traditionally dealt only with (first-order) preferences, that is, those that are revealed by agents as they buy goods and services. The complex psychological and cultural processes that lie behind the actually observed market choices have generally been considered the business of psychologists, sociologists, and anthropologists.

There were some good reasons for this self-denying ordinance. Nevertheless, one aspect in the formation of choice and preference must be of concern to the economist, to the extent that he claims an interest in understanding processes of economic change. That aspect has nothing to do with the cultural condi-

---

[1]See Schelling, p. 342, and Sen, p. 335.

tioning of tastes and choice behavior, at least at a first level of inquiry; its starting point is rather a very general observation on human nature (and should therefore be congenial to economics with its eighteenth-century moorings): men and women have the ability to step back from their "revealed" wants, volitions, and preferences, to ask themselves whether they really want these wants and prefer these preferences and, consequently, to form metapreferences that may differ from their preferences. Unsurprisingly, it was a philosopher who first put matters this way. Harry Frankfurt argued that this ability to step back is unique in humans, but is not present in all of them. Those who lack this ability he called "wantons": they are entirely, unreflectively, in the grip of their whims and passions. (The terminology is quite apt as it conforms to common usage: wanton murder is precisely murder "for no good reason," i.e., murder that has not been preceded by the formation of any metapreference for murder.)

It is easy to see that there is a close link between preference change and the concept of metapreferences; for, as I have pointed out before, certainty about the existence of metapreferences can only be gained through changes in actual choice behavior. If preferences and metapreferences always coincide, so that the agent is permanently at peace with himself no matter what choices he makes, then the metapreferences hardly lead an independent existence and are mere shadows of the preferences. If, on the other hand, the two kinds of preference are permanently at odds, so that the agent always acts against his better judgment, then again, the metapreference cannot only be dismissed as wholly ineffective, but doubts will arise whether it is really there at all. In such cases, the situation is best characterized as a "tie-in purchase": along with the preferred commodity the consumer insists on acquiring unhappiness, regret, and guilt over having preferred it.

The notion of metapreference does not tell us much about the way actual change in choice behavior comes about. The battle to impose the metapreference is fought out within the self and is marked by all kinds of advances and reverses as well as by ruses and strategic devices. I am not concerned here with this topic, which Schelling has made his own, only with pointing out that an occasional success in changing choice behavior is essential for validating the concept of metapreferences.

Conversely, this concept illuminates the varied nature of preference change, for it is now possible to distinguish between two kinds of preference changes. One is the reflective and tortuous kind, preceded as it is by the formation of a metapreference at odds with the observed and hitherto practiced preference. But preference changes also take place without any elaborate antecedent development of metapreferences. Following Frankfurt's terminology, the unreflective changes in preferences might be called wanton. These are the preference changes economists have primarily focused on: impulsive, uncomplicated, haphazard, publicity-induced, and generally minor (apples vs. pears) changes in tastes. In contrast, the nonwanton change of preference is not really a change in tastes at all. A taste is almost defined as a preference about which you do not argue—*de gustibus non est disputandum*. A taste about which you argue, with others *or yourself*, ceases ipso facto being a taste—it turns into a *value*. When a change in preferences has been preceded by the formation of a metapreference, much argument has obviously gone on within the divided self; it typically represents a change in values rather than a change in tastes.

Given the economists' concentration on, and consequent bias for, wanton preference changes, changes of the reflective kind have tended to be downgraded to the wanton kind by assimilating them to changes in tastes: thus Becker ascribed patterns of discriminatory hiring to a "taste for discrimination," and Johnson similarly analyzed increases in protectionism as reflecting an enhanced "taste for nationalism." Such interpretations strike me as objectionable on two counts: first, they impede a serious intellectual effort to understand what are strongly held values and difficult to achieve changes in values rather than tastes and changes in tastes; second, the illusion is fostered that raising the cost of discrimination (or nationalism) is the simple and sovereign policy instrument for getting people to indulge less in those odd "tastes."

There is a more general point here. Economists often propose to deal with unethical or antisocial behavior by raising the cost of that behavior rather than by proclaiming standards and imposing prohibitions and sanctions. The reason is probably that they think of citizens as consumers with unchanging or arbitrarily changing tastes in matters of civic as well as commodity-oriented behavior. This view tends to neglect the possibility that people are capable of changing their values. A principal purpose of publicly proclaimed laws and regulations is to stigmatize antisocial behavior and thereby to influence citizens' values and behavior codes. This educational, value-molding function of the law is as important as its deterrent and repressive functions.[2] Accordingly, as Kelman has shown, the resistance of legislators to the economists' proposals to deal with pollution exclusively through effluent charges and similar devices becomes intelligible and, up to a point, defensible.[3] The propensity to pollute of industrialists and corporations is not necessarily like a fixed demand schedule, so that all one can do is to make them pay their way for the pollution they are presumed to be bent on causing: that propensity is likely to be affected (the demand curve could shift) as a result of a general change in the civic climate that is signaled—in part—by the proclamation of laws and regulations against pollution.

In the light of the distinction between wanton and nonwanton preference changes, or between changes in tastes and changes in values, it also becomes possible to understand—and to criticize—the recent attempt of Becker and Stigler to do without the notion of preference changes for the purpose of explaining changes in behavior. Equating preference changes to changes in what they themselves call "inscrutable, often capricious tastes," they find, quite rightly, any changes in those kinds of tastes (our wanton changes) of little analytical interest.[4] But in their sub-

---

[2] "Lawgivers make the citizen good by inculcating [good] habits in them, and this is the aim of every lawgiver; if he does not succeed in doing that, his legislation is a failure. It is in this that a good constitution differs from a bad one." Aristotle, *Nicomachean Ethics*, 1103b.

[3] See Kelman, pp. 44–53.

[4] See Becker and Stigler, p. 76.

sequent determination to explain all behavior change through price and income differences, they neglect one important source of such change: autonomous, reflective change in values. For example, in their analysis of beneficial and harmful addiction they take the elasticity of the individual's demand curve for music or heroin as given and, it would seem, immutable. May I urge that changes in values do occur from time to time in the lives of individuals, within generations, and from one generation to another, and that those changes and their effects on behavior are worth exploring—that, in brief, *de valoribus est disputandum?*

TWO KINDS OF ACTIVITIES

From consumption I now turn to production and to human activites such as work and effort involved in achieving production goals. Much of economic activity is directed to the production of (private) goods and services that are then sold in the market. From the point of view of the firm, the activity carries with it a neat distinction between process and outcome, inputs and outputs, or costs and revenue. From the point of view of the individual participant in the process, a seemingly similar distinction can be drawn between work and pay or between effort and reward. Yet there is a well-known difference between the firm and the individual: for the firm any outlay is unambiguously to be entered on the negative side of the accounts whereas work can be more or less irksome or pleasant—even the same work can be felt as more pleasant by the same person from one day to the next. This problem, in particular its positive and normative consequences for income differentials, has attracted the attention of a long line of economists starting with Adam Smith. Most recently Winston has drawn a distinction between "process utility" and "goal utility," making it clear that the means to the end of productive effort need not be entered on the negative side in a calculus of satisfaction.[5] At the same time, this distinction keeps

---

[5]See Winston, pp. 193–97.

intact the basic instrumental conception of work, the means-end dichotomy on which our understanding of the work and production process has been essentially—and, up to a point, so usefully—based.

But there is a need to go further if the complexity and full range of human activities, productive and otherwise, are to be appreciated. Once again, more structure would be helpful. The possible existence of wholly *noninstrumental* activities is suggested by everyday language, which speaks of activities that are undertaken "for their own sake" and that "carry their own reward." These are somewhat trite, unconvincing phrases: after all, any sustained activity, with the possible exception of pure play, is undertaken with some idea about an intended outcome. A person who claims to be working exclusively for the sake of the rewards yielded by the exertion itself is usually suspect of hypocrisy: one feels he is really after the money, the advancement, or—at the least—the glory, and thus is an instrumentalist after all.

Some progress can be made with the matter by looking at the varying predictability of the intended outcome of different productive activities. Certain activities, typically of a routine character, have perfectly predictable outcomes. With regard to such tasks, there is no doubt in the individual's mind that effort will yield the anticipated outcome—an hour of labor will yield the well-known, fully visualized result as well as entitle the worker, if he has been contracted for the job, to a wage that can be used for the purchase of desired (and usually also well-known) goods. Under these conditions, the separation of the process into means and ends, or into costs and benefits, occurs almost spontaneously and work appears to assume a wholly instrumental character.

But there are many kinds of activities, from that of a research scientist to that of a composer or an advocate of some public policy, whose intended outcome cannot be relied upon to materialize with certainty. Among these activities there are some—applied laboratory research may be an example—whose outcome cannot be predicted for any single day or month; nevertheless, success in achieving the intended result steadily gains in likelihood as the time of work is extended. In this case, the uncertainty is probabilistic, and one can speak of a certainty equivalent with regard to the output of the activity in any given period so that, once again, the separation of the process into means and ends is experienced, and work of this sort largely retains its instrumental cast. The combination of uncertainty about the result of work for a short stretch of time with near certainty of achievement over a longer period confers to these kinds of nonroutine activities an especially attractive, "stimulating," "exciting" quality that tends to be absent both from wholly routine activities whose outcome never fails to materialize no matter how short the work period, and from very different kinds of nonroutine activities, to be discussed presently.

From their earliest origins, men and women appear to have allocated time to undertakings whose success is simply unpredictable: the pursuit of truth, beauty, justice, liberty, community, friendship, love, salvation, and so on. As a rule, these pursuits are, of course, carried on through a variety of exertions for apparently limited and specific objectives (writing a book, participating in a political campaign, etc.). Nevertheless, an important component of the activities thus undertaken is best described not as labor or work, but as *striving*—a term that precisely intimates the lack of a reliable relation between effort and result. A means-end or cost-benefit calculus is impossible under the circumstances.

These activities have sometimes been referred to, in contrast to the instrumental ones, as "affective" or "expressive."[6] But labeling them does not contribute a great deal to understanding them, for the question is really why such activities should be taken up at all. It is important to note that by no means are these activities always pleasant in themselves; in fact, some of them are sure to be quite strenuous or highly dangerous. Do we have here, then, another paradox or puzzle, one that relates not just to voting (why do rational people bother to vote?) but to a much wider and most vital group of activities? I suppose we do—from

[6]See Smelser, and Parsons (cited by Smelser).

the point of view of instrumental reason, noninstrumental action is bound to be something of a mystery. But I have proposed an at least semirational explanation: these noninstrumental activities whose outcome is so uncertain are strangely characterized by a certain fusion of (and confusion between) striving and attaining.

According to conventional economic thinking, utility accrues to an individual primarily upon reaching the goal of consumption, that is, in the process of actually consuming a good or enjoying its use. But given our lively imagination, things are really rather more complicated. When we become sure that some desired good is actually going to be ours or that some desired event is definitely going to happen—be it a good meal, a meeting with the beloved, or the awarding of an honor—we experience the well-known pleasure of *savoring* that future event in advance (the term *savoring* was suggested to me by George Loewenstein). Moreover, this premature hauling in of utility is not limited to situations where the future event is near and certain, or is believed to be so. When the goal is distant and its attainment quite problematic, something very much like savoring can occur, provided a determined personal quest is undertaken. He who strives after truth (or beauty) frequently experiences the conviction, fleeting though it may be, that he has found (or achieved) it. He who participates in a movement for liberty or justice frequently has the experience of already bringing these ideals within reach. In Pascal's formation:

> The hope Christians have to possess an infinite good is mixed with actual enjoyment . . . for they are not like those people who would hope for a kingdom of which they, as subjects, have nothing; rather, they hope for holiness, and for freedom from injustice, and they partake of both.[7]

This savoring, this fusion of striving and attaining, is a fact of experience that goes far to account for the existence and importance of noninstrumental activities. As though in compen-

---

[7]See Pascal, 540.

sation for the uncertainty about the outcome, and for the strenuousness or dangerousness of the activity, the striving effort is colored by the goal and in this fashion makes for an experience that is very different from merely agreeable, pleasurable, or even stimulating: in spite of its frequently painful character it has a well-known, intoxicating quality.

The foregoing interpretation of noninstrumental action is complemented by an alternative view which has been proposed by the sociologist Pizzorno. For him, participation in politics is often engaged in because it enhances one's feeling of belonging to a group. I would add that noninstrumental action in general makes one feel more human. Such action can then be considered, in economic terms, as an *investment in individual and group identity*. In lieu of Pascal, those who advocate this alternative way of explaining noninstrumental action might invoke Jean-Paul Sartre as their patron saint, given the following lines from Sartre's posthumously published wartime diary:

> Throughout his enterprises [man] aims not at self-preservation, as has often been said, or at self-aggrandizement; rather, he seeks to *found* himself. And at the end of every one of these enterprises, he finds that he is back where he started: purposeless, through and through. Hence those well-known disappointments subsequent to effort, to triumph, to love.[8]

In other words, the feeling of having achieved belongingness and personhood is likely to be just as evanescent as the fusion of striving and attaining which I stressed earlier. The two views are related attempts at achieving an uncommonly difficult insight: to think instrumentally about the noninstrumental.

But why should economics be concerned with all this? Is it not enough for this discipline to attempt an adequate account of man's instrumental activities—a vast area indeed—while leaving the other, somewhat murky regions alone? Up to a point such a limitation makes sense. But as economics grows more ambitious, it becomes of increasing importance to appreciate that the means-

---

[8]See Sartre, p. 141; my emphasis.

end, cost-benefit model is far from covering all aspects of human activity and experience.

Take the analysis of political action, an area in which economists have become interested as a natural extension of their work on public goods. Here the neglect of the noninstrumental mode of action was responsible for the inability of the economic approach to understand why people bother to vote and why they engage from time to time in collective action. Once the noninstrumental mode is paid some attention, it becomes possible to account for these otherwise puzzling phenomena. It is the fusion of striving and attaining, as well as the urge to invest in individual or group identity, that leads to a conclusion exactly opposite to the "free ride" argument with respect to collective action: As I wrote in *Shifting Involvements,* "since the output and objective of collective action are . . . a public good available to all, the only way an individual can raise the benefit accruing to him from the collective action is by stepping up *his own input,* his effort on behalf of the public policy he espouses. Far from shirking and attempting to get a free ride, a truly maximizing individual will attempt to be as activist as he can manage."

The preceding argument does not imply, of course, that citizens will never adopt the instrumental mode of action with respect to action in the public interest. On the contrary, quite a few may well move from one mode to the other, and such oscillations could help explain the observed instability both of individual commitment and of many social movements.

A better understanding of collective action is by no means the only benefit that stands to flow from a more open attitude toward the possibility of noninstrumental action. As I have argued earlier, a strong affinity exists between instrumental and routine activities on the one hand, and between noninstrumental and nonroutine activities on the other. But just as I noted the existence of nonroutine activities that are predominantly instrumental (in the case of an applied research laboratory), so can routine work have more or less of a noninstrumental component, as Veblen stressed in *The Instinct of Workmanship.* Lately the conviction has gained ground that fluctuations in this component must be drawn upon to account for variations in labor productivity and for shifts in industrial leadership. It does make a great deal of difference, so it seems, whether people look at their work as "just a job" or also as part of some collective celebration.

Contact can now be made with my earlier plea for complicating the analysis of choice behavior with the concept of meta-preferences. One important application of this concept can precisely be found in an individual's deliberation whether to devote more of his time and energy to instrumental activities at the expense of the noninstrumental ones, or vice versa. Shifts of this sort may mean an actual shift from one kind of activity to another (e.g., from public action to private pursuits); they will often involve a two-stage sequence in which an actor first decides to look, say, at some public involvement through instrumental rather than noninstrumental lenses, and then comes to feel that he should cut down on the public activity or give it up altogether. Quite possibly, what I was really after (or should have been after) in *Shifting Involvements* was to describe an oscillation between the instrumental and noninstrumental modes of action, with the pursuits of the private and of the public happiness serving as concrete manifestations of these two basic modes.

"LOVE": NEITHER SCARCE RESOURCE NOR AUGMENTABLE SKILL

My next plea for complicating economic discourse also deals with the production side, but more specifically with the role of one important prerequisite or ingredient known variously as morality, civic spirit, trust, observance of elementary ethical norms, and so on. The need of any functioning economic system for this "input" is widely recognized. But disagreement exists over what happens to this "input" as it is used.

There are essentially two opposite models of factor use. The traditional one is constructed on the basis of given, depletable resources that get incorporated into the product. The scarcer the resource the higher its price and the less of it will be used by the economizing firm in combination with other inputs. Arrow's more recent model recognizes the possibility of "learning by doing"; use of a resource such as a skill has the immediate effect of improving the skill, of enlarging (rather than depleting) its availability. The recognition of this sort of process—a considerable, strangely belated insight—also leads to important unorthodox policy conclusions, such as the desirability of subsidizing certain "scarce" inputs, since a subsidy-induced increase in their use will lead to the increased supply which, according to the more traditional model, was expected to be produced on the contrary by raising their price. I shall now attempt to show that neither of these two models is able to deal adequately with the nature of the factor of production that is under discussion here.

Because the "scarce resource" model has long been dominant, it has been extended to domains where its validity is highly dubious. Some thirty years ago, Robertson wrote a characteristically witty paper entitled "What Does the Economist Economize?" His often cited answer was: love, which he called "that scarce resource." Robertson explained, through a number of well-chosen illustrations from the contemporary economic scene, that it was the economist's job to create an institutional environment and pattern of motivation where as small a burden as possible would be placed, for the purposes of society's functioning, on this thing called "love," a term he used as a shortcut for morality and civic spirit. In so arguing, he was of course at one with Adam Smith, who celebrated society's ability to do without "benevolence" (of the butcher, brewer, and baker) as long as individual "interest" was given full scope. Robertson does not invoke Smith, quoting instead a telling phrase by Alfred Marshall: "Progress chiefly depends on the extent to which the *strongest* and not merely the *highest* forces of human nature can be utilized for the increase of social good."[9] This is yet another way of asserting that the social order is more secure when it is built on interest rather than on love or benevolence. But the sharpness of Robertson's

---

[9] See Robertson, pp. 154, 148.

own formulation makes it possible to identify the flaw in this recurrent mode of reasoning.

Once love and particularly public morality are equated with a scarce resource, the need to economize it seems self-evident. Yet a moment's reflection is enough to realize that the analogy is not only questionable but a bit absurd—and therefore funny. Take, for example, the well-known case of the person who drives in the morning rush hour and quips, upon yielding to another motorist: "I have done my good deed for the day; for the remainder, I can now act like a bastard." What strikes one as funny and absurd here is precisely the assumption, on the part of our driver, that he comes equipped with a strictly limited supply of good deeds; that, in other words, love should be treated as a scarce resource—as Robertson claimed. We know instinctively that the supply of such resources as love or public spirit is not fixed or limited as may be the case for other factors of production. The analogy is faulty for two reasons: first of all, these are resources whose supply may well increase rather than decrease through use; second, these resources do not remain intact if they stay unused—like the ability to speak a foreign language or to play the piano, these moral resources are likely to become depleted and to atrophy if not used.

In a first approximation, then, Robertson's prescription appears to be founded on a confusion between the *use of a resource* and the *practice of an ability*. While human abilities and skills are valuable economic resources, most of them respond positively to practice, in a learning-by-doing manner, and negatively to nonpractice. (Just a few skills—swimming and bicycle riding come to mind—seem to stay at the same level in spite of prolonged nonpractice: once acquired, it is virtually impossible to lose or forget them. In counterpart, such skills often are not notably improved beyond one's level by practice.)

It was on the basis of this atrophy dynamic—the less the requirements of the social order for public spirit, the more the supply of public spirit dries up—that the United States' system for obtaining an adequate supply of human blood for medical purposes, with its only partial reliance on voluntary giving, was criticized by the British sociologist Richard Titmuss. And the British policial economist Fred Hirsch generalized the point: once a social system, such as capitalism, convinces everyone that it can dispense with morality and public spirit, the universal pursuit of self-interest being all that is needed for satisfactory performance, the system will undermine its own viability, which is in fact premised on civic behavior and on the respect of certain moral norms to a far greater extent than capitalism's official ideology avows.

How is it possible to reconcile the concerns of Titmuss and Hirsch with those seemingly opposite, yet surely not without some foundation, of Robertson, Smith, and Marshall? The truth is that, in his fondness for paradox, Robertson did his position a disservice: he opened his flank to easy attack when he equated love with some factor of production in strictly limited supply that needs to be economized. But what about the alternative analogy that equates love, benevolence, and public spirit with a skill that is improved through practice and atrophies without it? This, too, has its weak points. Whereas public spirit will atrophy if too few demands are made upon it, it is not at all certain that the practice of benevolence will indefinitely have a positive feedback effect on the supply of this "skill." The practice of benevolence yields satisfaction ("makes you feel good"), to be sure, and therefore feeds upon itself up to a point, but this process is very different from practicing a manual (or intellectual) skill: here the practice leads to greater *dexterity*, which is usually a net addition to one's abilities, that is, it is not acquired at the expense of some other skill or ability. In the case of benevolence, on the other hand, the point is soon reached where increased practice does conflict with self-interest and even self-preservation: our quipping motorist, to go back to him, has not exhausted his daily supply of benevolence by yielding once, but there surely will be *some* limit to his benevolent driving behavior, in deference to his own vital—perhaps even ethically compelling—displacement needs.

Robertson had a point, therefore, when he maintained that there could be institutional arrangements that make excessive demands on civic behavior, just as Titmuss and Hirsch were right in pointing to the opposite danger: the possibility that society makes insufficient demands on civic spirit. In both cases, there is a shortfall in public spirit, but in the cases pointed to by Robertson et al., the remedy consists in institutional arrangements placing less reliance on civic spirit and more on self-interest, whereas in the situations that have caught the attention of Titmuss and Hirsch, there is need for increased emphasis on, and practice of, community values and benevolence. These two parties argue along exactly opposite lines, but both have a point. Love, benevolence, and civic spirit neither are scarce factors in fixed supply nor do they act like skills and abilities that improve and expand more or less indefinitely with practice. Rather, they exhibit a complex, composite behavior: they atrophy when not adequately practiced and appealed to by the ruling socioeconomic regime, yet will once again make themselves scarce when preached and relied on to excess.

To make matters worse, the precise location of these two danger zones—which, incidentally, may correspond roughly to the complementary ills of today's capitalist and centrally planned societies—is by no means known, nor are these zones ever stable. An ideological-institutional regime that in wartime or other times of stress and public fervor is ideally suited to call forth the energies and efforts of the citizenry is well advised to give way to another that appeals more to private interest and less to civic spirit in a subsequent, less exalted period. Inversely, a regime of the latter sort may, because of the ensuing "atrophy of public meanings,"[10] give rise to anomie and unwillingness ever to sacrifice private or group interest to the public weal so that a move back to a more community-oriented regime would be called for.

CONCLUSION

I promised to inquire whether the various complications of traditional concepts that have been proposed have any common

---

[10]Taylor, p. 123.

structure. The answer should be obvious: all these complications flow from a single source—the incredible complexity of human nature, which was disregarded by traditional theory for very good reason but which must be spoon-fed back into the traditional findings for the sake of greater realism.

A plea to recognize this complexity was implicit in my earlier insistence that "voice" be granted a role in certain economic processes alongside "exit," or competition. The efficient economic agent of traditional theory is essentially a silent-scanner and "superior statistician," as Arrow put it, whereas I argued that she also has considerable gifts of verbal and nonverbal communication and persuasion that will enable her to affect economic processes.

Another fundamental characteristic of humans is that they are self-evaluating beings, perhaps the only ones among living organisms. This simple fact forces the intrusion of metapreferences into the theory of consumer choice and makes it possible to distinguish between two fundamentally different kinds of preference changes. The self-evaluating function may be considered a variant of the communication or voice function: it also consists in a person addressing, criticizing, or persuading someone, but this someone is now the self rather than a supplier or an organization to which one belongs. But let us beware of excessive parsimony!

In addition to being endowed with such capabilities as communication, persuasion, and self-evaluation, humanity is beset by a number of fundamental, unresolved, and perhaps unresolvable tensions. A tension of this kind is that between instrumental and noninstrumental modes of behavior and action. Economics has, for very good reasons, concentrated wholly on the instrumental mode. I plead here for a concern with the opposite mode, on the grounds that it is not wholly impervious to economic reasoning; and that it helps us understand matters that have been found puzzling, such as collective action and shifts in labor productivity.

Finally, I have turned to another basic tension humanity must live with, this one resulting from the fact that we live in society.

It is the tension between self and others, between self-interest, on the one hand, and public morality, service to community, or even self-sacrifice, on the other, or between "interest" and "benevolence" as Adam Smith put it. Here again, economics has concentrated overwhelmingly on one term of the dichotomy, while putting forward simplistic and contradictory propositions on how to deal with the other. The contradiction can be resolved by closer attention to the special nature of public morality as an "input."

In sum, I have complicated economic discourse by attempting to incorporate into it two basic human endowments and two basic tensions that are part of the human condition. To my mind, this is just a beginning.

Bibliographical References

Aristotle. *Nicomachean Ethics*. Translated by Martin Ostwald. Indianapolis: Bobbs-Merrill, 1962.

Arrow, Kenneth J. "The Economic Implications of Learning by Doing." *Review of Economic Studies* 29 (1962): 155–73.

———. "The Future and the Present in Economic Life." *Economic Inquiry* 16: (1978): 160.

Becker, Gary S. *The Economies of Discrimination*. Chicago: Chicago University Press, 1957.

Becker, Gary S., and Stigler, George. "De Gustibus Non Est Disputandum." *American Economic Review* 67 (1977): 76–90.

Frankfurt, Harry G. "Freedom of the Will and the Concept of a Person." *Journal of Philosophy* 68 (1971): 5–20.

Hirsch, Fred. *Social Limits to Growth*. Cambridge, Mass.: Harvard University Press, 1976.

Hirschman, Albert O. *Exit, Voice, and Loyalty: Responses to Decline in Firms, Organizations, and States*. Cambridge, Mass.: Harvard University Press, 1970.

———. *Shifting Involvements: Private Interest and Public Action*. Princeton, N.J.: Princeton University Press, 1982.

Johnson, Harry G. "A Theoretical Model of Economic Nationalism in New and Developing States." *Political Science Quarterly* 80 (1965); 169–85.

Kelman, Steven. *What Price Incentives? Economists and the Environment*. Boston, Mass.: Auburn House, 1981.

Loewenstein, George F. "Expectations and Intertemporal Choice." Ph. D. Diss., Department of Economics, Yale University, 1985.

Parsons, Talcott. "Toward a Common Language for the Area of Social Science." In *Essays in Sociological Theory, Pure and Applied*. Glencoe, Ill.: Free Press, 1949.

———. "Pattern Variables Revisited." *American Sociological Review* 25 (1960): 467–83.

Pascal, Blaise. *Pensées*. Brunschvicg edition.

Pizzorno, Alessandro. "Sulla razionalità della scelta democratica." *Stato e Mercato* (1983): 3–46; English version in *Telos*. Spring 1985.

Robertson, Dennis H. "What Does the Economist Economize?" In *Economic Commentaries*, pp. 147–55. London: Staples Press, 1956.

Sartre, Jean-Paul. *Les Carnets de la drôle de guerre*. Paris: Gallimard, 1983.

Schelling, Thomas C. *Choice and Consequence*. Cambridge, Mass.: Harvard University Press, 1984.

Sen, Amartya K. "Rational Fools: A Critique of the Behavioral Foundations of Economic Theory." *Philosophy and Public Affairs* 6 (1977): 317–44.

Smelser, Neil J. "Vicissitudes of Work and Love in Anglo-American Society." In *Themes of Work and Love in Adulthood*, edited by Neil J. Smelser and Erik H. Erikson, pp. 105–19. Cambridge, Mass.: Harvard University Press, 1980.

Taylor, Charles. *The Pattern of Politics*. Toronto: McClelland and Stewart, 1970.

Titmuss, Richard M. *The Gift Relationship*. London: Allen and Unwin, 1970.

Veblen, Thorstein. *The Instinct of Workmanship and the State of the Industrial Arts*. New York: Macmillan, 1914.

Winston, Gordon C. *The Timing of Economic Activities*. Cambridge: Cambridge University Press, 1982.

PART III

7. The Welfare State in Trouble:

STRUCTURAL CRISIS · OR GROWING PAINS?

We all know about persons who are complacent: they gloss over an important flaw in the functioning of something—a human body, a marriage, an economic policy, or a society—and try hard to convince themselves and others that nothing is really wrong; if they advocate any action, once the symptoms of trouble can no longer be ignored, they will typically prescribe aspirin when radical surgery is required. What about a term for the opposite fault: a term, that is, that would designate a person who forever diagnoses basic disorder and prescribes radical cures when the difficulty at hand may well take care of itself in time or calls only for mild intervention? I propose, for want of a more compact term, the "structuralist (or fundamentalist) fallacy," since those who are affected by this trait always speak of structural problems and the need for fundamental remedies.

Economists have long arrayed themselves into the two camps that are implicit in the two opposite faults just noted: those who are convinced that every departure from equilibrium is likely to be temporary and requires only a bit of clever management (if anything) have long been battling it out with those who are just as certain that such a departure signals a deep malady and per-haps the final crisis of the system. Naturally enough, the former turn out, from time to time, to be complacent while the latter will on occasion commit the structuralist fallacy. Being rather bored by both ideological camps, I tend to shift from one to the other depending on whom I am talking to. Given the complexity and ambiguity of the real world, a useful function may actually be served by such contrary behavior as I now hope to show by looking at the so-called "crisis of the welfare state."

That the welfare state is in trouble can hardly be contested. Considerable difficulties are presently experienced in the West in extending or even maintaining the social accomplishments of recent decades. Hostility toward some of the services provided is widespread, even among the beneficiaries. A political reaction has already occurred in some of the countries (Sweden, United Kingdom) that have gone furthest along the welfare-state road. In the United States, Proposition 13 and assorted phenomena have generally come under the label of "tax revolt"; to an important extent, this revolt is not a purely self-serving act on the part of the taxpayer but arises from a growing lack of confidence in the state's abilities to "solve" social problems. This lack of confidence can in turn be traced to recent experiences in social engineering (for example, the War on Poverty) and their alleged failure.

A number of explanations are offered for the difficulties the welfare state is running into, and most of them are of the structuralist kind. Long ago, Colin Clark alleged that in the capitalist system a fairly rigid limit was set on the ability to divert factor income for purposes of expanding social services and other public expenditures: the system would stop working (that is, capitalists would no longer invest, workers' productivity would fall off, etc.) if that level were exceeded. The inability of the system to stand more than a certain level of transfer payments was thereby declared to be one of its structural properties. Widely espoused at first by conservatives, this structuralist thesis was given a Marxist tinge in O'Connor's *The Fiscal Crisis of the State*, which explained this crisis in terms of the underlying clash between two basic functions of the capitalist state, that is, between the need to assure continuing capital accumulation, on the one hand, and the imperatives of legitimation through some redistribution of income, on the other.

Subsequently, Habermas worked O'Connor's thesis into a more general argument under the exalted title *Legitimationsprobleme im Spätkapitalismus* (published in English as *Legitimation Crisis*). From there the argument passed back to the conservative or neoconservative camp which stirred up, in the mid-1970s, a considerable debate around issues of "governability of the democracies" and "governmental overload." Once again, the absolute and relative expansion of public expenditures for health, education, and welfare, which Samuel Huntington called the "welfare shift," was viewed as an important ingredient of a widely proclaimed "crisis of democracy."[1]

A very different explanation why the welfare state is in disrepute if not in crisis is implicit in Hirsch's argument in *The Social Limits to Growth*. According to this work, the difficulty about increasing social spending beyond a certain point does not originate only among those who are made to pay for it; to an important extent, it arises from the unhappiness of those whom the spending was supposed to benefit. The reasoning is based on the concept of "positional goods," which are desired less for their own sake than for the social rank and distinction they are expected to confer. Recently governments have been getting into the business of supplying such goods on a mass basis. In education, for example, certain diplomas have become more widely available, but for that reason their possession no longer leads to a better paying job or higher social position. As a result, the recipients of the publicly provided services are likely to be disgruntled and cannot be counted on to support the expansion of public spending and social services.

Once again we have here an argument of a structural kind. It is now the frustration of its very clients that explains the crisis of the welfare state, whereas the earlier conservative and neo-Marxist theories stressed the adverse reactions of the suppliers of investment capital. Both arguments see the expansion of the welfare state as creating a contradiction with basic characteristics of economy and society: the ensuing crisis is of a "fundamental" nature and requires "radical" remedies if it can be solved at all.

I shall now suggest an alternative explanation. Like the Fred

---

[1]See Crozier.

Hirsch thesis, it concentrates on the experience of those to whom the new government-supplied goods and services are made available. But it sees their disgruntled reaction not as a consequence of disappointment over the inability of these goods to satisfy their social ambitions. It can be argued more simply that a rapid expansion of the supply of certain goods and services is likely to bring with it a deterioration in their quality in relation to expectations, and that it is this quality decline which produces disaffection with the performance of the public sector. If this argument has merit, the problem is not all that fundamental, for the quality decline may well be temporary.

The idea that an expansion in output will be detrimental to product quality is a priori plausible, but has not, as far as I know, been subjected to a great deal of economic analysis, in contrast to the enormous attention that has been lavished on the effect of increasing output on unit cost. It is the old story of the neglect of the qualitative. An obviously interesting question is: when will an expansion of output caused by increasing demand be accompanied by a significant decline in quality? In line with this question one might define output elasticity of quality which would measure the response of quality to an increase in output within some stated time interval. Like the price elasticity of demand, this elasticity would normally have a negative sign with a limit of zero for those goods whose quality is totally unaffected by output increase. The output elasticity of quality is likely to be strongly related to the substitutability of inputs. If all input coefficients are rigidly fixed, an identical article, be it an umbrella or an airplane, is always being produced and quality cannot deteriorate as output is expanded. The possibility of deterioration opens up when one input or factor can be substituted for another.

The smooth isoquant of the textbook is of course drawn on the assumption that an increase in the use of one factor makes up *totally*, insofar as quality of the product is concerned, for the decreased use (in relative terms) of another. Actually it happens all the time that some factor or input substitution made to satisfy an expanding demand (one factor or input being in inelastic supply) results in a product that is not up to the traditional standards. Factor and input substitutability thus open the door to quality deterioration, whereas fixed coefficients make for invariant quality. Since substitutability is the rule in the world of neoclassical economics, it may be surprising that changes in the quality of output have not been given more attention. The reason is another pervasive assumption: that consumers have perfect information or learn instantly in a competitive market, immediately adjust their demand when faced with an inferior product or enforce an appropriate relative price reduction for it. In the real world, of course, input shifts and the resulting quality deterioration are often combined with noncompetitive markets, consumer ignorance, and slow learning about the changed characteristics of the product. It is my contention that this combination of circumstances is precisely characteristic of certain social services whose expansion in response to widespread demands has been considerable in recent decades.

Education is a pertinent example. On the production side, this "article" has a particularly high tolerance for quality decline and low-level performance, as expanded educational services can be and often are offered in spite of various unresolved bottlenecks—unprepared teachers, impossibly crowded classrooms, inadequate library and laboratory facilities, and so on. Educational services are in fact an extreme illustration of the possibility of quality decline that originates in a lopsided increase in inputs: it would be quite unthinkable to market similarly defective refrigerators or airplane services.

The latitude for quality decline is also related to the demand or consumption side. Consumers are poorly informed about the quality of the expanded services of an educational system and have few alternatives to choose from. Nevertheless, if the newly offered services are in fact defective, the result will eventually be widespread disappointment and discontent. The damage inflicted by having received a poor education is not easily undone: unlike apples, education is not bought recurrently in small quantities. The result is a kind of disappointment that cannot be easily extinguished by doing the right thing next time in the market and that therefore will lead a life of its own—with some possibly serious social and political consequences.

The welfare state may thus face a wave of hostile public opinion and as a result may well pass through a difficult phase, with the need to consolidate and even retrench.

However, if the reasons suggested here for the change in the climate of opinion are correct, the trouble may be temporary. The loss of popularity is connected with the decline in quality, which in turn is due to temporary factors, such as the rapid increase in supply. Once the new services can count on an adequately expanded base of inputs, the quality decline—seen as the basis for public disenchantment with the welfare state—should be duly reversed, and the social advances consolidated in fact as well as with public opinion. Over the long term, in other words, the output elasticity of quality is likely to be closer to zero than over the short term.

This "nonfundamental" diagnosis of the present difficulties of the welfare state is reinforced by some further observations. In the first place, when certain social services like education are expanded so as to cater to newly emerging groups, it may not be appropriate to offer exactly the same services as have previously been supplied. Hence, even without quality decline, and precisely because there has been no change or adaptation, the services might be ineffective and meet with criticism and resistance. Again a period of learning and mutual adjustment will be needed. Second, there has been a tendency in recent years for the demand for certain services to arise in advance of real knowledge of how to satisfy it; examples are day-care facilities and psychotherapeutic services. What happens in these situations is that suppliers only begin to learn on the job, in the process of rendering these newly popular services as best they can. A great deal has been written by Arrow, Akerlof, and others about consumer ignorance and the resulting asymmetrical situation of consumer and producer. In the present case, producers and suppliers of services are just as ignorant as consumers, at least during the earlier stages of their operation, and this accounts for the poor quality of services rendered and for the consequent disappointment of the consumer. Here, also, a learning process will take place, eventually leading to better-quality service and to more correct consumer expectations.

In sum, the difficulties of the welfare state can be interpreted, in part at least, as growing pains rather than as signs of systemic crisis.

To conclude, I wish to raise a question in the sociology of knowledge: why have the various conceivable nonstructural arguments not been coherently put forward so far, with the result that we could only choose between various kinds of structuralist explanations? The reason, I think, lies in a rather odd ideological asymmetry. In explaining it briefly I return to my introductory remarks on structuralist vs. nonstructuralist approaches to problem solving. Structuralist thinking about a problem or crisis comes easily to those who dislike the institution that experiences the problem or finds itself in crisis. For example, right-wing and conservative people dislike the welfare state and oppose its expansion: they are naturally prone to interpret any difficulties it encounters as symptoms of a deep-seated malady and as signals that radical retrenchment is in order. For similar reasons, left-wing and liberal opinion has traditionally opted for structuralist explanations when it came to account for difficulties experienced by capitalism. But with the debate about capitalism and the market economy having stood in the center of public discussion for so long, this tradition appears to have created on the Left something of an unthinking structuralist reflex: Left-liberal people are automatically partial to structuralist explanations, even though ideological self-interest ought to make them diagnose some difficulties—those that affect structures they themselves have promoted—as self-correcting or temporary. As a result of this strange ideological trap into which the Left has been falling, there has been a marked lack of balance in the analysis of the current difficulties of the welfare state.

Bibliographical References

Crozier, Michel, et al. *The Crisis of Democracy: Report on the Governability of Democracies to the Trilateral Commission.* New York: New York University Press, 1975.

Habermas, Jürgen. *Legitimationsprobleme im Spätkapitalismus.* Translated by Thomas McCarthy as *Legitimation Crisis.* Boston: Beacon Press, 1975.

Hirsch, Fred. *Social Limits to Growth.* Cambridge, Mass.: Harvard University Press, 1976.

O'Connor, James. *The Fiscal Crisis of the State.* New York: St. Martin's Press, 1973.

8. In Defense of Possibilism

Under what conditions is a revolution likely to have a democratic and when is it going to have an authoritarian outcome? The tradition of comparative sociological-historical inquiry established by Barrington Moore and carried forward by Theda Skocpol and others consists in looking for answers to such questions into what might be called "deep structure"—property relations and characteristics of the state. To the contrary, Shmuel Eisenstadt proposes to go back, if not to Geertz's "thick description," then to what the Annales school in France used to call rather contemptuously *l'histoire événementielle*—the history of events (which, incidentally, is now in the process of being rehabilitated by such luminaries as Emmanuel Leroy-Ladurie and Paul Ricoeur).

Personally, I am quite comfortable with this turn of the wheel or with this return to a once dominant point of view. Following in detail the process of a revolution gives us a strong feeling, as the structuralist approach does not, for the many might-have-beens of history, for narrowly and disastrously missed opportunities as well as for felicitous and surprising escapes from disaster; as a result, the event-minded historian is less likely than the sociologist to declare that, given such and such a structural condition, the outcome was preordained. With his emphasis on the

This note originated as a comment on a paper given by Shmuel N. Eisenstadt on "Outcomes of Revolutions: Autocracy vs. Democracy" and presented at a conference on the Limits of Democracy held in Rome in 1980 in memory of Gino Germani. See also Acknowledgments, p. 188.

revolutionary process, Eisenstadt in effect promises to restore a few degrees of freedom we were in danger of losing to the structuralists.

My complaint is that he does not really keep his promise. Let us take a look at the generalizations he snatches from a comparative look at revolutionary processes. Autocratic or authoritarian outcomes of revolutions, so he concludes after his survey, are more likely the more rigid and exclusive the prerevolutionary power holders were, and the more coercive the revolutionaries are in the course of the revolutionary process once they achieve power. This sounds disarmingly, even boringly obvious, but just for that reason we must be on our guard. Is it really true that the least coercive, that is, the gentlest revolutions are always best for a democratic outcome? As soon as that question is asked, what comes to my mind is the so-called German Revolution of 1918–19 which was of course far too gentle in leaving imperial Germany's socioeconomic, bureaucratic, and even military structures virtually untouched—as was graphically expressed in the book title *Der Kaiser ging, die Generäle blieben* (The Kaiser went, the generals stayed on). There can be no doubt that this gentleness of the revolution laid the groundwork for the later resurgence of nationalist forces and eventually for the Nazi takeover.

The German counterexample therefore suggests a first crude modification of Eisenstadt's rule. It looks as though the chances of a democratic outcome of a revolution might stand in some sort of curvilinear relationship to the thoroughness and violence of a revolution: too little thoroughness is just as bad as too much, that is, you need a minimum of thoroughness to avoid a vicious counterrevolution. But as it is impossible to know how much is too much (or how little, too little), this is an unhelpful way to look at the matter. One might propose, then, to complicate the model by introducing a second independent variable: the accomplishments of revolutions. Obviously, it is difficult to give a precise definition—different people will have very different ideas on what constitutes an accomplishment, but we all know there *is* such a thing. By focusing on coerciveness and dislocation Eisenstadt singles out the cost side of revolutions to the neglect of the benefit side. Perhaps it is possible to look at the democratic outcome of revolutions in terms of the favorable ratio of their accomplishments to their cost. In addition, one would probably want to specify that accomplishments must reach some minimum level, while the costs cannot exceed some ceiling without dooming the chances for a happy end. This would yield a more complex but, I believe, also a more realistic model. It would specify autocratic outcomes both when coerciveness is considerable no matter how large the accomplishments, and when accomplishments are meager no matter how low the degree of coerciveness. For a democratic outcome, on the other hand, substantial accomplishments must be combined with restraint with regard to coercion and violence. Accordingly, any revolution searching for a democratic or pluralist outcome must travel along a quite narrow path, but that proposition, being eminently realistic, only confirms the reformulation I have attempted.

There is a more fundamental reason why I am dissatisfied with the Eisenstadt approach. He tells us that the chances for a revolution to have a democratic outcome are poor if the prerevolutionary power holders are rigid and exclusive. So what are the many countries where the latter situation prevails supposed to do? Get themselves a different kind of elite? Or forgo any attempt to bring about change? What is at fault here, in my opinion, is the traditional probabilistic approach of the sociologist. Eisenstadt's proposition no doubt represents an important first insight and "lesson of history." But one cannot let matters rest there. The dismal conclusion (which is nothing but a variant of Myrdal's law of cumulative causation about the rich always getting richer and vice versa) must be complemented by what in my book *A Bias for Hope* I called "possibilism." In the present instance this consists in the discovery of paths, however narrow, leading to an outcome that appears to be foreclosed on the basis of probabilistic reasoning alone. History and historians are usually in charge of making such discoveries that contradict their own "lessons." But occasionally sociologists could come upon them also, if only they were attentive to the intersections of their numerous probabilistic statements.

To illustrate: not long ago I attended a conference on processes of "redemocratization," or, more modestly, on the possible transformation of authoritarian, autocratic regimes in Latin America and Latin Europe in the pluralist direction. One of the more interesting attempts at generalization put forward at the conference was the proposition that, for the transition to be successful, the moderate Right rather than the Left should win the first free elections after the "turn to pluralism"—a euphemism for the usually tumultuous period following the overthrow, demise, or death of the autocrat. This is in itself no easy trick to perform, but to make things even more complicated, another analyst came forward with a second general proposition based on a comparative survey of several cases: to gain strength and take root, the new pluralist regime should effect some changes that go beyond political liberalization; for example, it should at some point demonstrate that it can assert the national interest against foreign or multinational interference, or it should take some measures in the direction of greater social justice, such as land reform. The idea here is similar to the earlier one about revolutionary accomplishments being important for democratic outcomes.

Putting together these two conditions spells out once again a very narrow path for any successful transition to pluralism and democracy: one conceivable scenario is that the Left would first be briefly powerful, carry out some irreversible structural changes or "accomplishments," and then withdraw as a result of an election that would bring to power more moderate political forces. It is a considerable puzzle and paradox, but I believe it to be true that the spelling out of such fortuitous and a priori quite unlikely combinations of favorable circumstances or fortunate sequences is less discouraging than laying down overriding preconditions for redemocratization. The reason why the improbable sequence turns out to be subjectively hopeful is that it conjures up the image of a rare conjunction of circumstances *such as we are familiar with from history*. The mere act of finding or imagining such a conjunction gives confidence that, even if this particular one cannot be repeated or translated into reality, there must be some other similarly farfetched ones that history has up its sleeve. For history is nothing if not farfetched—unfortunately, one must add, in the direction of both good and evil.

9. Notes on Consolidating Democracy in Latin America

1. The point of departure of any serious thought about the chances for the consolidation of democracy in Latin America must surely be pessimism.[1] The principal reason is simply that the historical record is so unpromising. In this respect, the recent disintegration of seemingly well-entrenched authoritarian regimes in Argentina, Brazil, and Uruguay, and the apparent vigor of the new democratic currents in these countries are not necessarily encouraging. It looks as though the pervasive characteristic of *any* political regime in the more developed Latin American countries is instability: it affects even authoritarian political forms.

2. There is little point in looking for the root cause of this instability. Its strength and duration suggest that all kinds of convergent, interrelated factors are at work, from culture and social structure to economic vulnerability. It is correspondingly futile to lay down "preconditions" for consolidating democracy: they would merely serve to spell out a wholly utopian scheme for changing everything that has been characteristic of Latin American reality, and would therefore amount to wishing away that reality.

3. One particularly pernicious way of thinking about the con-

---

[1]This article was originally written for a meeting of social scientists held in São Paulo in December 1985 to explore problems of democratic consolidation in Latin America. See also Acknowledgments, p. 188.

solidation of democracy—a way that is likely to make a contribution to deconsolidation and has done so in the past—is to lay down strict conditions that need to be fulfilled if democracy is to have a chance, such as: dynamic economic growth must be resumed, income distribution must be improved, national autonomy must be asserted, political parties must show a cooperative spirit, the press and other media must be responsible, everyday relations between people must be restructured, etc. I submit that it is far more constructive to think about ways in which democracy may survive and become stronger in the face of, and in spite of, a series of continuing adverse situations or developments in many of these respects.

4. The inference that must be drawn from all this goes against the grain of much social-scientific thinking: instead of looking for necessary and sufficient conditions of change we must train ourselves to be on the lookout for unusual historical developments, rare constellations of favorable events, narrow paths, partial advances that may conceivably be followed by others, and the like. We must think of the possible rather than of the probable.

5. Here are three ways in which we can train ourselves to think about these matters:

(a) It may be useful to envisage the possibility of a disjunction between political and economic conditions that were thought of as being indissolubly linked. Ever since the destruction of the fragile Weimar and Spanish democracies in the 1930s, it has been axiomatic that an impairment of economic health will be fatal for a fledgling democracy. More recent experiences have shown, however, that at different historical times the connection is much less tight. The new democratic regimes of Spain and Portugal have so far weathered quite well the serious economic disturbances that followed the second oil shock of 1978 and the world recession between 1981 and 1983. This recession was particularly sharp in Brazil, leading to unprecedented levels of industrial unemployment in a country where there is no protection against this hazard; nevertheless, the political "opening" that was initiated by the military regime in 1974 proceeded undisturbed and was followed by the present phase of "democratization," during which censorship has been lifted and political power has been gradually returned to elected bodies and officials. The final step in the long process will be the election of a president by popular vote, for the first time in more than twenty years—the date of this event is yet to be set.

(b) One must even envisage the possibility of going forward in a pattern I have called "sailing against the wind."[2] Given two highly desirable goals, such as a polity with consolidated democratic institutions and a more prosperous economy where wealth is more equally shared, it is conceivable that a given society can, at certain times, move in one of these desirable directions only at the cost of losing some ground in the other. Provided the movement is eventually reversed, progress can be achieved in both directions, but at any one time progress in one direction may be had only at the cost of retrogression in the other.

(c) I do not actually believe that the situation is so filled with dilemmas. While all good things do not necessarily go together, it seems unreasonable to assert that they never do. What is certain is that a country experiencing a birth or rebirth of democracy will find that among the many other conceivable changes that are desirable per se and would serve to strengthen democracy, some are more nearly within reach than others. The task is then to watch out for such differences (instead of holding on to preconceived notions about priorities) and to pursue with particular energy such opportunities as may open up. Thus, in the wake of the repressive regimes of the recent past, a reaction against authoritarian political forms and a desire for greater participation are now strong and widespread. Moreover, in Argentina, Uruguay, and Brazil many novel forms of mobilization and militancy have arisen, from groups advocating human rights in Argentina to the Catholic grassroots movements known as Comunidades Eclesiais de Base in Brazil. In this atmosphere, the climate may be favorable for introducing democratic values of tolerance

---

[2]The concept of disjunction is taken from Daniel Bell, *The Cultural Contradictions of Capitalism* (New York: Basic Books, 1976).

and openness to discussion not only into the political process, but into everyday patterns of behavior among groups and individuals.[3]

6. This may then be a propitious time to reflect on the nature of values whose diffusion in the society is important for the consolidation of democracy. I shall briefly call attention to two recent contributions in this field which I see as complementary. The University of Chicago political scientist Adam Przeworski has pointed out in an article, entitled in its Portuguese version "Love Uncertainty and You Will Be Democratic" (*Novos Estudos CEBRAP,* July 1984), that one basic difference between democracy and authoritarianism is that, in the former, uncertainty about the course of policy-making is a conspicuous characteristic of the regime, since that course depends on the uncertain outcomes of popular elections.

In an authoritarian regime, certainty about future policy-making is of course not complete either, but there is much greater assurance about the kinds of policies and directions that will never be adopted. So accepting uncertainty about whether one's own program will be realized is an essential democratic virtue: I must value democracy more highly than the realization of specific programs and reforms, however fundamental I may judge them to be for further progress, democratic, economic, or otherwise.

7. Under what circumstances is this democratic virtue, this "love of uncertainty," likely to come into existence? A minimal condition is that the citizenry acquire a measure of patience. Suppose there are two parties that have staked out very different positions on all outstanding issues. If democracy is to be maintained after an election, the defeated party must be willing to wait for the next election instead of beginning to plot a coup, a guerrilla movement, or a revolution. With this proviso, society could have a democratic experience while remaining split into

---

[3]See two recent papers on this topic by Guillermo O'Donnell, "Democracia en la Argentina: micro y macro," and "Y a mi, que me importa? Sociabilidad y autoritarismo en Argentina y Brasil," working papers Nos. 2 and 9 (December 1983 and January 1984), Kellogg Institute, University of Notre Dame.

two or more antagonistic camps and without anyone ever changing his or her opinions.[4] The principles to which the actors subscribe may enable them—or so they firmly believe—to hold fully articulated positions on all present and even future policy issues, outside and in advance of any common deliberation, election campaign, or policy-making process. One senses, nevertheless, that a society whose activist members are so sure of where they stand, and so immune to outside argument, may find it difficult to abide by the democratic process. For this reason, the chances of survival of democracy will be improved if more demanding conditions than a mere increase in patience are met.

8. According to the French political theorist Bernard Manin, a genuine democratic political process implies that many of the people participating in it have only an approximate and somewhat uncertain initial opinion on various issues of public policy.[5] Notwithstanding the air of certainty with which candidates for office announce their views, full-fledged positions of many voters and policymakers emerge only as an actual debate and protracted deliberations about the issues take place as part of the electoral and legislative processes. A principal function of these debates is to develop new information as well as new arguments. As a result, final positions may well be at some distance from the ones initially held—and not only as a result of political compromise with opposing forces.

To Przeworski's acceptance of the uncertainty of outcomes Manin thus adds as a characteristic of democracy a degree of uncertainty on the part of citizens about the proper course to take, or at least about the validity of their initial opinions on

---

[4]This kind of democracy has been aptly called adversary democracy by Jane J. Mansbridge in her book *Beyond Adversary Democracy* (New York: Basic Books, 1980).

[5]"Volonté générale ou délibération? Esquisse d'une théorie de la délibération politique," *Le Débat,* January 1985; forthcoming in English in *Political Theory.*

various issues. This uncertainty would be resolved only in the course of the deliberations that are carried on in various democratic forums.

Manin sees this uncertainty, this lack of commitment to an inflexible a priori position, and the resulting deliberation about the proper course to pursue, as substitutes for the utopian, Rousseauian, requirement of unanimity of the popular will to establish the legitimacy of the democratic form of government. He therefore looks at uncertainty and at the deliberative process that follows more as an ideal to be approximated than as a rigid requirement for a democratic society.

This analysis is nevertheless illuminating for our purposes. It makes us realize that the total absence of this sort of uncertainty, the lack of openness to new information and to the opinions of others, is a real danger to the functioning of democratic society. Many cultures—including most Latin American ones I know—place considerable value on having strong opinions on virtually everything from the outset, and on winning an argument, rather than on listening and finding that something can occasionally be learned from others. To that extent, they are basically predisposed to an authoritarian rather than a democratic politics.

9. The matter can be put the following way: If a democratic regime is to have any chance at all of surviving, its citizens must accept Przeworski's uncertainty about outcomes, they must acquire a measure of patience. To become consolidated, the regime needs in addition some admixture of Manin's uncertainty, the awareness on the part of citizens that they are, and ought to be, somewhat tentative about what are the correct solutions to current problems in advance of any democratic debate. The prevailing culture may be strongly set against both kinds of uncertainty, but particularly against Manin's. The recent authoritarian regimes in Argentina, Brazil, and Uruguay can be understood in part as the final outcome of a politics where both of these uncertainties were wholly absent from the minds of the principal political actors. The current revulsion against those regimes could

imply a questioning of these mental habits, however deeply entrenched they may have been.

10. To become aware of an important mis-fit between a prevailing culture and the kinds of attitudes that are required for democracy is a step toward overcoming it. Providentially and un-Marxianly, refining our interpretation of the world means, in this instance, to begin to change it.

10. A Prototypical Economic Adviser:

JEAN GUSTAVE COURCELLE-SENEUIL

Jean Gustave Courcelle-Seneuil (1813–1892) was a French economist and economic adviser. Born in the Dordogne, he studied law in Paris, then returned to his native region to manage an industrial firm. At the same time, during the July Monarchy, he wrote for Republican newspapers and economic periodicals. After the 1848 Revolution, he briefly held a high position in the Ministry of Finance. In the following years, he became a frequent contributor to the *Journal des économistes* and published a successful textbook on banking in 1852. In 1853, the Chilean government contracted him to teach economics at the University of Chile in Santiago and to be available as an official economic adviser; he stayed for ten years, until 1863, when he returned to France. While in Chile, he published his most ambitious work in economics, the *Traité théorique et pratique d'économie politique* (1858), which the Chilean government arranged to bring out in a Spanish translation. After his return to France, he resumed his activity as prolific writer of books and articles dealing with economic affairs. He also published several works dealing with political and historical topics and translated into French John Stuart Mill's *Principles of Political Economy,* Sumner Maine's *Ancient Law,* and William Graham Sumner's *What Social Classes Owe to Each Other.* He was appointed councillor of state in 1879 and three years later was elected a member of the Académie des Sciences Morales et Politiques.

Throughout his life, Courcelle-Seneuil was a stalwart defender of free trade and laissez-faire. Charles Gide, the coauthor (with Charles Rist) of a well-known history of economic doctrines, wrote about him in rather sarcastic terms: "He was virtually the *pontifex maximus* of the classical school; the holy doctrines were entrusted to him and it was his vocation to denounce and exterminate the heretics. During many years he fulfilled this mission through book reviews in the *Journal des économistes* with priestly dignity. Argus-eyed, he knew how to detect the slightest deviations from the liberal school." Courcelle-Seneuil's special interest, starting with the publication of a small book on bank reform in 1840, was the introduction of more freedom into banking or, to use a modern term, the "deregulation" of this industry. Above all he advocated the abolition of the Bank of France's exclusive right of issue. According to Gide, Courcelle-Seneuil was esteemed more in England and the United States than in France. In any event, adoption of his monetary and banking proposals was never seriously considered in his own country.

Once in Chile, Courcelle-Seneuil became a powerful policymaker and influential teacher. He arrived at a time when the international prestige of the laissez-faire doctrine was at its height and when gold booms and subsequent busts in California and Australia caused considerable fluctuations in Chile's agricultural exports to these areas, creating a need for flexible short- and long-term credit facilities. This combination of events, joined with the prestige emanating from the foreign savant, permitted him to obtain in Chile what he had failed to achieve in his own country: under his guidance, the administration of Manuel Montt (1851–61) promulgated a banking law that established total freedom for any solvent person to found a bank and permitted all banks to issue currency subject only to one limitation: the bank notes in circulation were not to exceed 150 percent of the issuing bank's capital.

Courcelle-Seneuil's advice was also sought in connection with a new customs tariff, and here again he achieved substantial change: the level of protection was severely cut back, although some tariffs were retained for revenue purposes.

But the principal influence exercised by Courcelle-Seneuil

resided in his forceful teaching: as the University of Chile's first professor of economics, he was apparently successful in instilling doctrinaire zeal in his students, some of whom later became influential policymakers. Thus, Chilean historians not only have traced the abandonment of convertibility in 1878 to the permissiveness of the 1860 Banking Law and the lack of industrial development to the 1864 tariff, but also see Courcelle-Seneuil's indirect influence in the acquisition of the nitrate mines of Tarapacá by private foreign interests after Chile's victory over Peru in the War of the Pacific (1882) had given it title to the mines. Alienation of the mines was indeed recommended by a government committee dominated by Courcelle-Seneuil's disciples, who held, as their teacher did, that state ownership and management of business enterprises should be strictly shunned. Secular inflation, industrial backwardness, domination of the country's principal natural resources by foreigners—all of these protracted ills of the Chilean economy have been attributed to the French expert.

Since the economically advanced countries were also those where economic science first flourished, they soon produced a peculiar export product: the foreign economic expert or adviser. Courcelle-Seneuil is probably the earliest prototype of the genre, and his ironic career in Chile exhibits characteristics that were to remain typical of numerous later representatives. First, the adviser is deeply convinced that, thanks to the advances of economic science, he knows the correct solutions to economic problems no matter where they may arise. Second, the country that invites the expert looks forward to his advice as to some magic medicine that will work even when (perhaps especially when) it hurts. Some countries seem to be especially prone to this attitude. In Chile foreign or foreign-trained experts have played key roles at crisis junctures, from Courcelle-Seneuil at mid-nineteenth century to Edwin Kemmerer in the 1920s, the Klein-Saks Mission in the 1950s, and finally to the "Chicago boys" in the 1970s. Third, the influence of the adviser derives not only from the intrinsic value and persuasiveness of his message, but from the fact that he usually has good connections in his home country and therefore can facilitate access to its capital market. Courcelle-Seneuil, for example, suspended his university courses in 1858–59 to accompany a Chilean financial mission that traveled to France in search of a railroad construction loan. Fourth, the foreign adviser is often criticized for wishing to transplant the institutions of his own country to the country he advises, but his real ambition is more extravagant: it is to endow the country with those ideal institutions that exist in his mind only, for he has been unable to persuade his own countrymen to adopt them. Fifth, history in general, and nationalist historiography in particular, is likely to be unkind to the foreign adviser. In retrospect he can easily become a universal scapegoat: whatever went wrong is attributed to his nefarious influence. This demonization is more damaging than the adviser himself could possibly have been: it forestalls authentic learning from past experience.

Bibliographical References

Selected works by Courcelle-Seneuil: *Le Crédit et la banque*. Paris, 1840. *La Banque libre*. Paris: Guillaumin, 1867. *Traité théorique et pratique d'économie politique*. 2 vols. Paris: Amyot, 1867.

Encina, Francisco. *Historia de Chile*. Vol. 18, chap. 58. Santiago: Nascimiento, 1951.

Fuentealba H., Leonardo. *Courcelle-Seneuil en Chile: errores del liberalismo económico*. Santiago: Prensas de la Universidad de Chile, 1946.

Gide, Charles. "Die neuere volkswirtschaftliche Literatur Frankreichs." *Schmoller's Jahrbuch*, 1895.

Hirschman, Albert O. *Journeys toward Progress*. New York: Twentieth Century Fund, 1963, pp. 163–68.

Journal des économistes. July 1892. Obituaries.

Juglar, Clément. "Notice sur la vie et les travaux de M. J. G. Courcelle-Seneuil." Académie des Sciences Morales et Politiques, *Compte Rendu*, 1895, pp. 850–82.

Pinto S.C., Aníbal. *Chile, un caso de desarrollo frustrado*. Santiago: Editorial Universitaria, 1959.

Will, Robert M. "The Introduction of Classical Economics into Chile." *Hispanic-American Historical Review*, February 1964.

Acknowledgments

Chapter 1: Originally published in *Pioneers in Development,* edited by Gerald M. Meyer and Dudley Seers (New York: Oxford University Press, 1984). Copyright 1984 by the World Bank.

Chapters 2, 3, 4: These three chapters were written originally (1) as entries for *The New Palgrave, a Dictionary of Economic Theory and Doctrine,* to be published by the Macmillan Press Ltd., and (2) as lectures given (in French translation) at the Collège de France in May 1985, and to be published, together with chapter 6, by Les Editions de Minuit under the title *Pour une économie politique élargie.* I am grateful to Pierre Bourdieu, of the Collège de France, for his invitation. The texts published here are my original drafts for the Collège; they exceeded the space allowed by the editors of *The New Palgrave,* which will contain shortened versions.

Chapter 5: First published in English in the *Journal of Economic Literature* 20 (December 1982), and written originally for presentation as the fourth annual Marc Bloch Lecture under the auspices of the École des Hautes Études en Sciences Sociales on May 27, 1982, in Paris. It was also published, together with three other essays of mine, in *L'Économie comme science morale et politique* (Paris: Gallimard/Le Seuil, 1984). I am grateful to François Furet, then president of the École, for his invitation, and to Irwin L. Collier for able research assistance. As elsewhere in this book, translations are mine, unless otherwise noted.

Chapter 6: Originally written for a meeting of the American Academy of Arts and Sciences in Cambridge, Massachusetts, March 14, 1984, during which I was awarded the Academy's Talcott Parsons Prize for Excellence in the Social Sciences. Short versions were published in the *American Economic Review* 74 (May 1984), and in the *Bulletin* of the Academy 37 (May 1984). The complete version, printed here, was first published in *Economics and Philosophy* 1, no. 1 (1985).

Chapter 7: Originally published in *American Economic Review* 70 (May 1980), and reprinted in *Dissent*, Winter 1981.

Chapter 8: First published in Italian in *I limiti della democrazia,* edited by R. Scartezzini, L. Germani, and R. Gritti (Naples: Liguori, 1985), a volume that brings together papers presented at a conference on the Limits of Democracy held in Rome in 1980 in memory of Gino Germani.

Chapter 9: Reprinted with permission from *The New York Review of Books,* April 10, 1986. Copyright © 1986 Nyrev, Inc.

Chapter 10: Like chapters 2, 3, and 4, this one was originally written for *The New Palgrave*.

Index

DATE DUE

261-2500

Printed
in USA